CRYSTAL

HOPE YOU ENJOY THE

BOOK AS MUCH AS I~

WRITING IT

GREAT
NORTHERN
COCKTAILS

GREAT NORTHERN COCKTAILS

BY

SHAWN SOOLE

MIXELLANY

Photo credits: Alena Jenkins, 73; Brian Verch, 66; Elizabeth Gartside, 135; Kristopher Bahamondes & Zach Hoffman-Roger, 160; Michael Hall, 184; Rachel King, 123; Tom Scully, 146; World Class Canada, 77; Shutterstock, 28, 52, 89, 101, 115, 119, 128, 132, 153, 182

Mixellany books may be purchased for educational, business, or sales promotional use. For information contact: Mixellany Limited, The White House, Nettleton, Chippenham, Wiltshire SN14 7NS United Kingdom or email mixellanyltd@googlemail.com

First edition
ISBN 13:
(Hardcover) 978-1-907434-53-2; (Tradepaper) 978-1-907434-52-5

British Library Cataloguing in Publication Data. A catalogue record for this book is available from the British Library.

Dedicated to all the bartenders across Canada making a difference on the world stage.

Dedicated to the most understanding women in the world, Jillian and Mila Grace. Without you I wouldn't be able to achieve the things I strive for.

TABLE OF CONTENTS

INDEX
OF DRINKS

FOREWORD
Jeffrey Morgenthaler

IF MY MEMORY SERVES ME instead of fails me, as it often does, I met Shawn Soole sometime around the end of 2009. We'd been talking for years online about cocktails and bar-related stuff, but I'd never had the pleasure of meeting him in person.

He'd talked me into speaking at a little cocktail conference he was helping put on in Victoria, BC. I'd just landed in town after one of the most terrifying 20-minute seaplane flights I'd ever encountered, and was soon seated at his bar, which was conveniently located in my hotel.

Shawn is a formidable figure behind any bar. Somehow, he's both larger and louder than I am, which should come as a massive surprise to anyone who has ever met me and not yet had the pleasure of meeting Shawn. He also has one of those thick, obnoxious Australian accents, which was somehow less jarring than the plane flight I'd just suffered.

It would be impossible for anyone to remember much more from that night, because over the course of the next several hours he took me on a cocktail tour of Canada. Drinks were somehow materializing out of nowhere, bartenders were making guest appearances both behind the bar and at my side, and all the while Shawn was regaling me with stories from the Victoria bar scene and drink concepts he'd conceived of.

I've gotten to know Shawn pretty well since that night. I've spent many more nights like that first one sitting at his bar over the past decade. He's spent a few at mine. We've been in other cities together, too. Heck, we've even been to France together.

Shawn loves bartending more than just about anyone else I know. And he loves Canada, too. In the pages of this book you'll be immersed in those loves of his, and in your own way you'll get to go on that same journey I took with Shawn all those years ago. Try to remember as much as you can.

FOREWORD
PHILIP DUFF

I LOVE CANADA. I haven't seen all of it—you know it's enormous, right?—but I can always impress a Canadian by casually dropping into the conversation that I've actually been to Red Deer, Alberta. Because of my frequent visits, I can sympathize with laid-back Vancouverites about the stuck-up Torontonians, console the rootin' tootin' frontier inhabitants of Calgary on the topic of those strange-sounding denizens of Montreal, and shoot the breeze with locals in Halifax about how cold it is for this time of year, eh? I know what Tim's Bits, loonies and mickeys are (respectively, doughnut holes, a $1 coin and a 375ml flask of booze, which collectively lay the base for a good night out in Canada if you ask me). And I know its bars.

But not as well as Shawn Soole, an old friend of mine who first popped up on my radar many years ago when he was running successful bars in his native Australia. After emigrating to Victoria BC in Canada, he became one of its most famous adopted sons in the world of spirits, and—he's too modest to tell you this himself—put the country on the global cocktail map with a firm Australian bang.

The beverage programs he ran in BC garnered Canada's first-ever Tales of the Cocktail Spirited Awards (the liquid Oscars) nominations. Then the book he wrote did as well. Then he did, too. He helped resurrect the Toronto cocktail. He has travelled the world talking about cocktails and Canada. Everyone knows Shawn, and because of that, everyone knows Canada and its bartenders a little better, too. The book you hold in your hands will only continue Shawn's work to spread the word.

Canada has a history of spirits, drinking, cocktails and bar culture as rich as any in the world. Even state monopolies can't stop Canadians drinking! In the last 200 years cocktail culture has had its ups and downs, but we are now well into the Second Golden Age of Cocktails and there has never been a better time to drink in Canada. Get to know the history, the techniques and the bartenders and their fine drinks showcased in this book. Then, the next time you stroll into a nice bar in Edmonton or Niagara Falls or Winnipeg, order the best-sounding cocktail on the menu and, just before you raise it to your lips, raise a toast to the bartenders of Canada. It is their time.

INTRODUCTION

I WAS YOUNG AND SPRITELY when I moved to Canada from Australia in 2006; coming from a cocktail background, I landed in Victoria, British Columbia without knowing exactly what the town had to offer. My first job was at a franchise restaurant, something completely alien to me, given that these styles of restaurants are few and far between in Australia.

My first order to come in behind this new bar in a new country was an Americano. I was excited, seeing a classic cocktail ordered on my first day was something that made me giddy as I built it. Placed lovingly on the pass, I awaited the server to show her the Americano that was gently collecting condensation. She looked down and asked, "what is this?", I answered proud with a Cheshire Cat grin on my face, "an Americano". She looked at me in dismay and then began to explain what an Americano means in Canada. Deflated, I binned the Americano and began to make what most Canadians know as an Americano: A shot of espresso in hot water.

All those years ago, I could never believe that cocktail culture would be so expansive, inclusive and deep as it is today. I have been fortunate enough to travel the world and sing the praises and virtues of Canadian cocktail culture. The turning point for me was when I took over Clive's Classic Lounge in 2009, a newly renovated downtown hotel bar in the Chateau Victoria. Lushly appointed with leather, Swarovski crystal and dark wood, it screamed classic European hotel bar and so that's the direction we took it.

Taking over Clive's wasn't an easy endeavour by any stretch of the imagination, but it was one of my most rewarding. The beginning of social media opened up our little cocktail bar in a city of 100,000 people to a global audience, and in 2011 and 2012 we were nominated as Top 4 International Hotel Bar of the Year at Tales of the Cocktail's Spirited Awards. This was a huge achievement, one that I still relish, even after I moved on to work on projects like Little Jumbo, Café Mexico, OLO and Foxtrot Tango Whiskey Bar.

My love for this industry is never-ending, and Canada has not only found its way with its cocktail culture, it has been gaining a reputation on the global stage as a juggernaut that should be shown more attention. The Diageo World Class cocktail competition has had a definite influence, with 2015 Canadian champion Lauren Mote (of Bittered Sling bitters, plus everything else she does) and 2017 world champion Kaitlyn Stewart reigning supreme and also showing that it doesn't matter what sex, race or culture you come from to be some of the best in the world.

Great Northern Cocktails is my extended love letter to my adopted home country. Canada has shown the world just how resilient and amazing we can be.

We have all seen the magazine articles or the featured blog about the cocktail culture in major cities, showcasing the same roster of bartenders and their cocktails. This book has heavily featured a lot of this same roster, but I wanted to take it one step further.

In the beginning of my time in Victoria we were viewed as the underdogs, the fledglings pitted against the likes of Vancouver and Seattle. This was the case for many years, but little by little, we grew and became an entity unto ourselves. The Off the Beaten Path sections of this book are just that, celebrating one or two likeminded bartenders growing and nurturing a culture in the smallest, most unlikely of environments in the corners of Canada.

Showcasing big cities with a vibrant culture is equally as important as nurturing and featuring the wonderful and sometimes strenuous endeavours from a select few that see Canadian cocktail culture growing throughout the world.

SHAWN SOOLE ORIGINALS

MAYAHUEL FLAME***

2 oz (60 ml) reposado tequila (El Jimador)
½ oz (15 ml) Green tea and serrano chili amaro (p. 197)
2/3 oz (20 ml) Ginger & honey shrub (p. 196)
2/3 oz (20 ml) grapefruit juice

Glass: Stemless Wine / Old-Fashioned
Method: Shake all ingredients with ice and double-strain over an ice globe
Garnish: Fat grapefruit twist

DRUNK UNCLE*

1 ½ oz (45 ml) Islay whisky
¾ oz (22.5 ml) bianco vermouth (Martini)
¾ oz (22.5 ml) Cynar

Glass: Small Cocktail / Nick & Nora
Method: Stir all ingredients with ice and strain
Garnish: Grapefruit twist

FRAGOLA REGALE**

1 oz (30ml) rosé vermouth (Cocchi Rosa)
1 oz (30ml) Champagne strawberry acid(p. 191)
Top with prosecco

Glass: Highball / Collins
Method: Build over ice and stir
Garnish: Lemon twist

14

BARTENDING BASICS

Bartending is a skill that is not inherently natural to many people, it takes time and training to master the craft. However, like cooking, bartending is not hard. It is all a system of various tasks performed at the exact time to layer flavour and apply techniques to a final product. If you are an at-home bartender, you may watch your local bartender or YouTube videos; if you are looking at bartending as a career, it's about asking questions, watching techniques and practice, lots of practice. What follows are the basic outlines that we bartenders work within. In this industry, there are a lot of guidelines that can be stretched—or rewritten. That said, when it comes to the basics of bartending, there are some hard and fast rules.

COMPONENTS

BITTERS: Bitters in essence are your cocktail "spice rack", created using high-proof alcohol or glycerol infused with aromatics and flavoured with herbal essences. Dashes of different bitters can drastically change the drink you use them in, bringing out different flavours from the same spirits. Most old-school recipes only call for three styles of bitters: Angostura aromatic, Peychaud's, and orange bitters, such as Angostura or Regans' Orange Bitters No. 6. These are accessible, readily available and all you need if you are an at-home beginner. For professionals and enthusiasts, a wide array of bitters can be purchased these days. The Bitter Truth, Bittermens, Bittered Sling, and Ms. Better's Bitters are all good-quality bitters brands available online. If you want to create your own bitters at home, there are blogs that should be able to guide the way.

ICE: Ice is imperative in a properly made cocktail, it should be seen as the main ingredient in any cocktail, as without it the cocktail doesn't exist. Evolving with your surroundings is essential to an optimally chilled cocktail. If you have horrible slushy ice, dilution will be quick as well as chilling. The "best" ice is solid, 1¼-inch (3.2 cm) cubes made by machines, such as Kold-Draft and Hoshizaki. For the home bartender, Amazon stocks a wide array of soft plastic ice trays ranging from inch by inch to king cubes (2 inch by 2 inch) to ice spears and everything in between.

JUICES: Juices are basic modifiers for a cocktail. Whether they are citrus or more interesting flavours such as pear, juices should be, for the most part, freshly squeezed. The fresher the better, especially when it comes to citrus. Fruit juice has a very short lifespan, as it begins to oxidize at a pretty steady rate from the moment you finish juicing. Some develop flavour changes while others change colour—citrus juice can lose its bite, while juice from pulpy fruits, like apples and pears, can brown. If you can't squeeze your juice fresh and must pre-squeeze or use a packaged product, here are some hints: If you pre-squeeze citrus, know that it has about six to eight hours before it is oxidized; pre-squeezed apple juice oxidizes much faster. If you buy packaged juice, look for one that's 100 percent juice, not from concentrate, and contains added citric acid. Citric acid is basically the essence of citrus juice concentrated and is an active preserving agent, akin to squeezing lemon juice over a banana to stop it from browning.

LIQUOR: Next to ice, liquor is the most essential part of the cocktail and covers a wide array of flavours, styles, colours, and prices. Depending on where you live, choice depends on cost to quality ratio; do your due research on each product before you buy and ask questions at the liquor store. When first purchasing a selection of spirits for home or your bar, keep in mind a few basics; some ingredients such as amari, certain rums, and whiskies simply can't be substituted. There are many classic recipes that call for specific brands such as Gosling's Rum having to be used in the Dark 'n' Stormy. Expensive isn't always best, in this modern world of bartending, the price of a bottle of liquor now covers the bottle design, marketing campaign, and public relations. The key is to identify and find the "bang for your buck" brands on the market, these are an at-home bartender's best weapon to practicing the craft. Always remember, it's not about the brand but the liquid inside. Finally, you should also consider how you are applying the spirit to the drinks you like. For example, don't use ultra-premium products if you like your drinks mixed with juice or cream; instead, use a nice mid-range product. The time when you should pick a premium product is when you are showcasing it in a strong, spirit-forward drink. With so many local products now on the market, keep in mind that every product has its place somewhere; it's not a one-size-fits-all market.

In terms of selection, the spirits every bartender requires are a good vodka (Stolichnaya or Absolut); a quality light rum and a quality dark rum (Havana Club, Flor de Caña or specifics like Gosling's for the Dark 'n' Stormy); a

Canadian rye whisky (Lot 40, Canadian Club 100% Rye or Forty Creek); a tequila (100 percent agave, such as Espolón; if you are picking an aged tequila, I find reposados more versatile); an old-school London dry gin for making G&Ts (Beefeater 24 or Tanqueray, though quality gins at a good price point are many); and finally, a Scotch whisky and a bourbon whiskey (head for a quality blended Scotch, such as Whyte & Mackay or The Famous Grouse, which will not be too smoky but plenty Scotchy, and for bourbon, pick up Maker's Mark or Bulleit). To round out this basic selection, add a sweet vermouth and a dry vermouth (Cinzano Rosso and Noilly Prat, respectively), and you'll have yourself the makings for a bank of cocktails that will keep you going for a few months. Once you have your base knowledge down, you can start expanding, maybe adding a bottle of Campari, Strega, or Chartreuse, which will further augment the range of drinks you can prepare.

SYRUPS: Syrups can be summed up with one rule: If you can only make it as good as but not better than you can buy it, then buy it; BG Reynolds and Small Hand Foods make amazing orgeat and falernum along with classics like raspberry and pineapple. Homemade syrups should be made only in batches that suit your needs. For example, making a big batch of rhubarb syrup and only using a couple of ounces is nonsensical. It will result in your batch fermenting and going off. Most syrups have a shelf life of two to four weeks before they start to lose flavour and turn. Take pulpy fruit like rhubarb and berries and freeze them; the internal membranes break when the water expands, which makes it easier to extract the juice and flavour from the defrosted fruit.

METHODS

BLENDING AND SLUSHIE MACHINES: Blending constantly comes in and out of favour with bartenders around the world. Blenders have their place behind the bar and, in the right hands, can produce amazing cocktails— especially in the tiki realm of drinks. Blending is an appropriate way of combining such ingredients with others to create a smooth, ready-to-serve mixture. When blended-drink recipes call for ice, you should use one scoop of ice per drink.

Slushie machines are one of the best modern re-adaptations out there. Outside the realm of most home bartenders, a well-made slushie machine drink is a thing of beauty. Speed of service, consistency and creativity are all positives in the bar world; while not the easiest recipes to develop, once they are perfected, they are divine.

BUILDING: Building is one of the simplest methods of making a cocktail. Ingredients are poured over ice and gently stirred to combine their flavours. Drinks such as the Negroni and the Old Fashioned are classic built drinks. This method is one that's easy to do but hard to perfect, trying to get the balance of dilution and chill.

MUDDLING: To muddle, place fruits, herbs, and/or vegetables in a shaker and press them with a muddler. Doing so extracts their flavours, aromatics, and juices and also adds an interesting dimension to the drink that other methods don't produce. If you don't have a muddler, the handle of a rolling pin will suffice.

RINSING / SPRITZING: To rinse a glass, pour a very small amount of the desired liquid into the glass; swirl the glass until the entire inside is lightly coated with liquid. This method benefits the olfactory sense, enhancing what you smell while controlling how much of a certain flavour comes out in the drink. Though it requires a special tool, the most effective way of rinsing a glass is to pour some of the liquid that you want to use into an atomizer and spray it on the inside. Doing so will give you better coverage while using less liquid. Spritzing is when you use an atomizer to coat both the inside and outside of the glass with a fine layer of liquid.

SHAKING: When a drink contains eggs, fruit juices, or dairy, it is necessary to shake the ingredients with ice. Shaking is the method in which you use a cocktail shaker to simultaneously emulsify and chill the cocktail. Shaking with ice is similar to a paint can being shaken at the hardware store—the rotation, the shaking speed, and the ice combine all the ingredients in such a way that they become a velvety, balanced, and chilled cocktail.

There are three kinds of shaking: Dry shaking is shaking without ice. This is done to emulsify the ingredients, particularly if the recipe calls for egg whites. Dry shaking is often followed with a wet shake to then chill the drink. Wet shaking is shaking with ice, and is most often carried out alone, but as mentioned can also follow a dry shake. And finally, hard shaking, a method made famous by many a Japanese bartender and dictates a hard, point-to-point shake with ice. Put simply, it is shaking the shaker as hard as you possibly can.

Ice is key in the shaking process: Your shaker should be two-thirds full of quality ice cubes. Hold both ends of the shaker tight. If you are using a Boston-style shaker, hold the glass away from your guests so that if it explodes, which it can, the contents will spray all over you and not your guests. Shake hard; this is not a baby or a bag of chips. You should feel the shaker get cold and the contents change from heavy, clunky blocks of ice to more liquid. When the shaker is almost too cold to hold, the drink is ready.

STIRRING: Stirring is one of the most original methods of cocktail creation. It's simple, effective, and can be difficult to master. The general rule is that anything spirit-forward should be stirred. Fill a mixing glass or tin two-thirds full of ice, add your ingredients, and stir with a good barspoon. Dilution and chilling are essential in a spirit-forward cocktail—too much dilution can ruin it, while not enough chilling means it will be warm. It takes some practice to get this balance perfect and to your taste, but it will become second nature once you have it down. You will need a Hawthorne or julep strainer to strain a stirred drink into your chosen glass.

STRAINING, DOUBLE-STRAINING, AND DIRTY/JUNK STRAINING: Straining has changed dramatically over the centuries. Some shakers, like the cobbler, have built-in strainers, while others, like the Boston and Parisian, do not and thus require the use of a Hawthorne or julep strainer. In any case, straining removes large ice cubes, muddled fruit, and any larger, unwanted particles that may be unsavoury to your guests. When it comes to double-straining, it's really a matter of personal preference, but the general rule of thumb is that drinks served in cocktail glasses should always be double strained through a combination of a Hawthorne or julep, teamed with a tea strainer or fine strainer, while drinks served on the rocks can be single-strained. Dirty straining isn't really straining at all. After you have shaken the drink, instead of straining it, you simply pour the contents into a clean glass.

GARNISHES

Decorating or garnishing a cocktail, especially in the modern cocktail world, can be done using just about anything but should always follow one rule: A garnish should add something to the drink. Whether it is a sprig of mint for olfactory purposes or a slice of lime to add acidity to the drink as you sip it, a garnish should always be purposeful. That said, it is important to avoid overpowering the drink. When garnishing with a slice of fruit, be careful with the size—too thin is flimsy while too thick can unbalance the look, and even the flavour, of the cocktail.

CITRUS PEEL SPIRAL: Use a parer or vegetable peeler to cut away the skin of a citrus fruit. Working in a circular motion, take care not to cut into the bitter pith.

CITRUS SLICE: One of the simplest and most effective garnishes is a thin slice of citrus (approximately 2 to 4 millimetres thick), which can be placed into the drink or, if you cut a slit in it, on the rim of the glass.

CITRUS TWIST: Cut a thin section of citrus fruit peel crosswise and then twist it. Serve on the side of a glass or in it.

COCKTAIL PICKS: Picks come in all shapes, sizes, and materials these days, from cheap bamboo and wood all the way up to expensive, reusable stainless steel. They are perfect for spearing olives, cherries, or small fruit garnishes.

FRESHLY GROUND NUTMEG OR CINNAMON: You can use powdered nutmeg or cinnamon on your cocktails, but it is best to grind the spices fresh, using a plain or specialized grinder.

FROSTING/RIMMING: Margaritas and other mixed drinks often call for the rim of the glass to be coated with sugar, salt, or another powdered ingredient. The common method of frosting or rimming is to first rub the rim of the glass with a slice of citrus fruit, then dip the very edge of the rim into a small bowl of sugar or salt. Make sure that only the outside of the glass is rimmed—no one wants salt or too much sugar in their drink.

MARASCHINO CHERRIES: All bars have maraschino cherries. But since the cocktail garnish market is very lucrative these days, you can get quality cherries (not the radioactive ones!) from many delis and specialty food purveyors. Look for non-bright red ones. An unnatural red colour is an unmistakable indicator of cherries that are chemically enhanced.

SPRIGS: Sprigs of mint or similar herbs have always been popular in cocktails. With any herb, especially mint, it is best to use a nice-sized sprig and give it a spank (or slap) —place the sprig into the palm of one hand and smack it with the back of your other hand. You can also gently scrunch the sprig in your hand. Doing so helps release the herb's essential oils and makes it an aromatic addition to the cocktail—and the first thing the customer will smell.

ZEST: When, for example, a recipe calls for the "zest from 1 lime," or other citrus fruit, the entire skin is required. On the other hand, "2 lime zests" are two sections of lime peel cut using a vegetable peeler. You should never grate the peel because too much pith will come away with the skin. Flaming a zest (usually the thicker skin from a citrus fruit like an orange or a lemon) adds a different flavour to the drink. The explosive burst of flame that results when the citrus oils ignite creates a deep, clean citrus aroma and flavour.

GLASSWARE

There are so many glasses in the world that every bartender drools over and every home bartender wants for their collection. However, the basic three that you really need for any bar are the "classics": An old-fashioned glass, a highball glass, and a large cocktail glass (or the unmentionable martini glass). Once you have stocked up, the number of cocktails you can make grows exponentially, and then you can concentrate on building the rest of your collection. The other glassware listed in this section are more "luxury" items that can be procured later on. Thrift and antique stores can be great sources for finding that special little something for your collection.

COCKTAIL GLASS—LARGE: This is where the infamous V-shaped martini glass comes into play. Usually a larger glass holding up to 12 ounces (350 ml), it can be found in pretty much every bar worldwide. Following the movement toward smaller glassware, the large cocktail glass seems to be shrinking down to a more appropriate size of 6 to 8 ounces (175–250 ml).

COCKTAIL GALSS—SMALL OR NICK & NORA: Said to have been modelled after Marie Antoinette's breasts, this small shallow cocktail glass (also known as a cocktail coupe) is around 5 ounces (145 ml) and never larger than 6 ounces (175 ml). More suitable for cocktails that are spirit-forward and well chilled. Whereas the Nick & Nora glass has gained popularity out of the late 2010s when the *Thin Man* movies (in which Nick and Nora are the leads played by William Powell and Myrna Loy) are deeper almost large egg cup shaped glasses.

FIZZ / SOUR GLASS: This shorter glass is perfect for fizzes. It also accommodates most sours flawlessly, as well as any drink shaken over ice and then strained without, with room to spare for a splash of soda. Though the much taller slim fizz glass is an uncommon piece of glassware in most bars, it is a great substitute if you don't want to use the usual flute for sparkling cocktails.

FLIP GLASS: The flip is an interchangeable drink that can be served in a variety of glassware. We tend to use a vintage-style glass for aesthetics, but you can use teacups, fizz glasses, etc.

FLUTE: The champagne flute is synonymous with high lifestyle and fine drinking. The flute should be 5 ounces (145 ml).

HIGHBALL / COLLINS GLASS: A classic highball is about 10 to 12 ounces (300–350 ml) and has a nice wide base. It's suitable for any highball cocktail or Collins.

JULEP MUG: A julep mug is a very specific piece of glassware for the bar. Shaped like a tankard, it is usually made of pewter to conduct the cold of the crushed ice that is used in classic julep-style drinks. It holds approximately 8 to 10 ounces (250–300 ml).

MASON JAR: A popular and cheap vessel for most at-home bars, these are great glasses for summer patio entertaining and especially cool, trendy tiki drinks. And anything goes with regards to size and style but try to stick with a wide mouth.

OLD-FASHIONED / ROCKS GLASS: A classic short glass that you will see used in most bars for mixed drinks and straight spirits on the rocks. The standard old-fashioned glass is 6 to 8 ounces (175–250 ml), but nowadays you can get double rocks glasses that are closer to 10 to 12 ounces (300–350 ml).

PORT GLASS: A port glass is a small, wine-glass-shaped glass that holds about 2 to 4 ounces (60–120 ml). It can be used to serve most fortified wines, such as madeira and sherry.

SNIFTER: The classic brandy snifter has begun sneaking onto cocktail menus worldwide. It can be used as an alternative to wine glasses or as an easier substitute for stemless wine glasses.

SPECIAL COFFEE MUG: Hot toddy mugs or special coffee mugs are the relatively standard, heavy glass mugs normally used to serve your Baileys coffee. They are thicker than regular mugs to keep the heat of the drink in. A nog glass—an insulated glass mug or cup used for serving egg nog—is an acceptable alternative.

TASTING GLASS / ISO: A smaller wine glass perfect for tasting spirits straight, trying a smaller pour of wine or beer, or having a spot of port or sherry. Tasting glasses can also be used as an alternative to traditional cocktail glasses. Bartenders are always looking for new ways to present their drinks and this glass is an increasingly popular choice.

TIKI MUG: These specialized, somewhat expensive ceramic mugs are moulded after various motifs of Polynesian tiki culture. They can range from 6 ounces (175 ml) to 12 ounces (350 ml).

WINE GLASS: The wine glass comes in many sizes. During the birth of the bartending craft, it held only a few ounces but now balloons out to a monster 15 to 20 ounces (450–600 ml). An appropriate size for serving spritzers, coolers, or sangria is about 8 to 12 ounces (250–350 ml).

WINE GLASS—STEMLESS: Self-explanatory: A wine glass with no stem. A bowl-shaped glass with a wide, flat base for stability. It looks great on a table with an ice globe, sugar rimmed, or decorated with a nice, fat hanging spiral of citrus peel.

Great bartenders adapt to their surroundings and evolve their style to whatever they have on hand. For example, you should be able to make a good cocktail with nothing but a Mason Jar and a teaspoon. But if you have access to great equipment, it will make your life so much better. The old adage that carpenters are only as good as their tools is very true for bartenders as well. However, the only tools you need at home to get started are a barspoon, some strainers, and a shaker tin. For bartenders wanting to build their collections, high-end barspoons, Japanese shakers, and jiggers are the next step—one that will showcase your personal style.

With online stores like Amazon and Cocktail Kingdom being easily accessible with great selections, the quality and quantity is purely up to you and your budget.

BAR KNIFE: A sharp knife about 4 to 8 inches (10–20 cm) long is the perfect length for everything from slicing citrus all the way up to dismantling a pineapple.

BARSPOON: This is a simple tool that is actually extremely specialized. A regular parfait or long spoon is fine for at-home use, but for the professional, a twisted-neck barspoon is necessary. The twists should be tight and should stretch from the base to the top, where a small flat disk or muddler is very handy.

BOSTON SHAKER: The simplest style of shaker: A two-piece shaker comprising a tin piece and a glass piece, although two tins have also become more popular in modern bartending. You build the drink in the pint-size glass, add ice with the tin half, tap, and shake with ice. Takes a bit of practice to open, but it is the most versatile of all the shakers.

CHANNEL KNIFE: An old-school tool, the channel knife cuts a clean, crisp channel into citrus. It is useful for making thin twists, which are perfect for more subtle glasses, such as flutes, that require a longer citrus spiral.

COBBLER SHAKER: One of the oldest and most common styles of shaker, this three-piece shaker has a built-in strainer. Sometimes the smallest cap section of the shaker is a jigger, used for measuring spirits on the go.

HAND JUICER: One of the most necessary pieces of equipment in the bar, there are two main sizes that you need: A medium-sized juicer for juicing lemons, limes, and oranges, and a large juicer for grapefruits. These are pretty much the only sizes you need.

HAWTHORNE STRAINER: The classic strainer that most bartenders have behind their bars, the Hawthorne has a tight spring around its perimeter. This makes it perfect to use with the tin portion of a Boston Shaker when straining shaken cocktails.

JIGGER—STANDARD: Jiggers are used for measuring liquid ingredients. The style of jigger used is a personal preference; some love the glowing copper hue of a Japanese jigger or the utilitarian nature of an OXO. Whatever you choose it should be able to measure ¼ oz (7.5 ml) up to 2 oz (60 ml) without too much fuss.

JULEP STRAINER: Looking somewhat like a kitchen strainer or skimmer, the julep strainer has made a resurgence in cocktail culture in the last few years. It fits perfectly into the glass portion of a Boston Shaker for stirred cocktails.

MUDDLER: The muddler was, until recently, a very important tool behind the bar; however, its popularity has slowly declined over the last few years. The best muddler for cocktails such as a Caipirinha is made of solid plastic or wood, is moulded to the hands, and at least 10 to 12 inches (25–30 cm) long. It also sometimes has a toothed base.

PARISIAN SHAKER: The latest trend on the cocktail scene, it's a slightly more cumbersome and complicated two-piece shaker that requires a certain level of skill to "crack" once chilled.

PEELER: A wide potato peeler is a perfect tool for every bar. It cuts perfect slices underneath the skin of citrus fruits without leaving any pith on the twists.

TEA STRAINER / DOUBLE STRAINER: When double-straining to remove pulp or ice shards, a fine tea strainer or "double strainer" is necessary. A simple tea strainer also works very well.

THE
DRINK-MAKING LEGEND

Throughout this book, recipes are classified with an asterisk (*) to indicate their level of difficulty.

Easy *
Perfect for first-timers or for big cocktail parties. These drinks use liquor that is readily available and are relatively easy to make.

Medium **
For the cocktail nerd or home bartender who wants to build on his or her skills, these drinks use house-made syrups, liquors, and bitters that may need to be tracked down.

Difficult ***
For experienced bartenders, these cocktails use more complex house-made syrups and extremely hard-to-find ingredients. The mixing methods are tricky as well.

BRITISH COLUMBIA

BRITISH COLUMBIA is one of the largest provinces in the country, measuring in at over seven times the size of the United Kingdom. This area stretches from the coastline of Vancouver and the islands to the snow-capped peaks of the Kootenays and everything else in between, with swaths of untouched forests dotted with small rural townships. British Columbia has a vibrant drinking culture thanks to decades of world-class wine making, the craft beer explosion of the 2010s and most recently the introduction of quality local spirits from the burgeoning craft spirit scene. This has fueled the cocktail scene in the major populaces of Vancouver and Victoria.

OFF THE BEATEN PATH:
VANCOUVER ISLAND

VANCOUVER ISLAND is off the far west coast of Canada, a scenic 45-minute sea plane ride from Vancouver takes you through the smaller islands that dot between the two coasts. With Victoria as its major hub, the long drive North crosses pine forests, picturesque beaches and towns that connect it all. The island has a lot to offer in the way of surfing on the western side in Tofino, to sport fishing in the far north. With wineries, cideries, distilleries, and breweries sprinkled around every major hub, the island gives you a diverse experience in the food and drink culture of this isolated place.

28

VICTORIA

VICTORIA is a small city with a big culture, with world-class bars and bartenders all working towards a common goal of giving the best experience to the very knowledgeable clientele. It all started at Solomon's in 2008; the first real cocktail bar to be opened in the capital by Solomon Siegel.

A few years after, the hotel bar ruled the scene—Veneto and Clive's Classic Lounge both housed in the Hotel Rialto and Chateau Victoria respectively took the mantle after Solomon's unfortunately closed. Both bars elevated and exposed Victoria's cocktail culture to the world, nurturing many young bartenders who would later disperse and create mini cocktail scenes in various bars throughout the city.

Victoria is always burgeoning, with a small population of under 200,000 people; the bar community will always be punching above its weight.

MARLEE BAXTER

Originally from the east, Marlee has been bartending since she attended university in Guelph, Ontario. Her fascination with cocktails started as a customer at Little Jumbo, where she learned the basics through consumption, trial, and error. She was given the opportunity to learn behind that bar as her first cocktail-focused bartending job and hasn't looked back since.

She believes that the best things in life are simple, and all the greatest cocktails are derivatives from the classics. Becoming part of the bartending community has been her favorite part of her career, especially given the tight knit nature of the Victoria scene.

WOODEN PEG***

1 oz (30 ml) blended whisky
(Monkey Shoulder)
1 ½ oz (45 ml) House-made
Drambuie (p. 198)

Glass: Old-Fashioned / Rocks
Method: Mix ingredients
together and age in American oak
barrel for 4 weeks. To serve, pour
2 ½ oz (75 ml) of aged cocktail
over clear ice chunk
Garnish: Lemon twist

JOSH BOUDREAU

Josh Boudreau began his professional bartending career in 2010 at the acclaimed Veneto Lounge in Victoria's heritage landmark Hotel Rialto. A charismatic performer and an eager newcomer to the reawakening of culinary-level cocktails and classicist service, Josh quickly excelled in his chosen trade, winning the locally-coveted title of Best Bartender in the Pacific Northwest in 2012 and again in 2013. He was named lead bartender at Veneto shortly thereafter and continued as an essential constituent of its success until 2018.

Josh started down his own mentorship path with Nimble Bar Company's professional bartending course in 2018. He led the cocktail program at Agrius, Victoria's celebrated organic farm-to-table restaurant, until his new adventure with the award-winning heli-skiing company Bella Coola Helisports. Josh also maintains an active role in the Canadian music industry as a theory and performance instructor, and as the lead guitarist for the esteemed rock ensemble Ellice Blackout.

ROOTS & BLUES**

2oz (60 ml) bourbon (Woodford Reserve)
½ oz (15 ml) Fernet-Branca
½ oz (15 ml) Roots & blues syrup (p. 204)

Glass: Small Cocktail / Nick & Nora
Method: Stir all ingredients with ice and strain
Garnish: Lemon twist

WEST BOURGET

West is a bartender who engages in hospitality for the love of the craft. Beginning in the service industry at 15, he worked his way steadily towards becoming a bartender, seeing the joy that they were capable of bringing to people. Unwilling to sacrifice creativity he strived to find a place in the food and beverage industry where cocktails were standard fare. When he found employment at Clive's Classic Lounge, it felt like a homecoming.

For the next eight months he worked under the tutelage of a man named Brendan Brewster, who will forever influence his service and drink-making style. His particular style is wildly varied. He has experimented heavily with the savoury side of cocktails, like tiki drinks with kimchi, and Dirty Martinis washed with anchovy paste. Through all of this, the drink that best represents his style though, is one that existed for a brief four months at the incomparable Foxtrot Tango Whiskey Bar. He now resides at the locally focussed, award-winning restaurant OLO in Victoria's Chinatown.

1 INCH PUNCH**

1 ½ oz (45 ml) Vanilla-infused rum (Appleton 12 year) (p. 209)
¾ oz (22.5 ml) brandy (Torres 5 year)
¾ oz (22.5 ml) Peach black tea oleo saccharum (p. 202)
½ oz (15 ml) lemon juice
½ oz (15 ml) water

Glass: Tea Cup and Saucer
Method: Stir all ingredients with ice and strain into glass
Garnish: Grated nutmeg and lemon channel

JANE CULPRIT

Jane has been fortunate enough to work for some of the great institutions in Victoria. Starting as a busser at Pagliacci's, she honed her bar skills slinging Shirley Temples, building Sangria, and shaking the odd drink while learning the fine art of hospitality. She then moved on to Cenote and worked under Scott Lansdowne. Most recently, she's proud to have developed the bar program at the brand-new Sherwood, where she manages and gets behind the wood from time to time.

In 2011, she co-founded Bonkers Empire, a collective committed to making cocktail culture more accessible and approachable. Through Bonkers, Jane and the team offer free education for anyone wanting to learn bar basics, operate a pop-up bar in unlikely places, and throws parties and fundraisers to benefit local arts and charity. Bonkers bartenders are famously theatrical, engaging and interactive. Drinks are always either free or cheap, in the interest of getting people to try new things without breaking the bank.

DARK ARTS**

½ oz (15 ml) amber rum (Flor de Cana 5 year)
½ oz (15 ml) Coffee-infused sweet vermouth (Bows and Arrows San Agustin Guatemala coffee bean-infused Cinzano) (p. 193)
¾ oz (22.5 ml) apricot brandy (Giffard)
½ oz (15 ml) lemon juice
1 dash Angostura bitters
1 dash Scrappy's cardamom bitters
1 oz (30 ml) soda

Glass: Old-Fashioned / Rocks
Method: Build over ice and stir
Garnish: Lemon twist

ALISHA FLEMING

Alisha started in the industry at Veneto when Solomon Siegel and Simon Ogden ran the bar and grew interested in cocktails. She had her first stage shift under the tutelage of Simon Ogden and later Solomon gave her a bartending job at Catalano, an expansive Spanish-inspired restaurant in downtown Victoria. She spent her first few months there learning everything she could from Solomon. After having a grounding in the cocktail industry, Alisha moved to other notable cocktail spots such as Cenote and Zambris; she has now found a solid tenure at Clive's Classic Lounge working with Jayce Noals.

THE KIPLING COCKTAIL*

1 ½ oz (45 ml) London dry gin (Bulldog)
½ oz (15 ml) maraschino (Luxardo)
½ oz (15 ml) orgeat (Giffard)
¾ oz (22.5 ml) lime juice
1 dash Fee Brothers Black Walnut Bitters

Glass: Small Cocktail / Nick & Nora
Method: Shake all ingredients with ice and double strain
Garnish: Lime leaf

AVI KUNEN

Avi entered adult life knowing next to nothing about drinks, notably buying a bottle of dry vermouth in Madrid because the label said "bianco" and he thought it was a very reasonably-priced white wine. Intending to pursue an athletic scholarship, Avi wanted a job that would allow him to work part-time, but make him decent money, so he enrolled in a two-week bartending course to learn, among other things, the difference between wine and vermouth.

His certificate got him a job at a small-town Legion bar, where he worked for a few months before using his knowledge of how to make a Negroni to trick a fine-dining restaurant into giving him a daytime bartending job. He spent the next few years learning how to serve people, design a good bar menu, and stir two drinks at once. Now Avi works at Little Jumbo, a high-volume cocktail bar and restaurant that lets him lean into the athletic side of bartending that he loves, while taking charge of a hyper-seasonal bar program that makes great drinks but takes things just seriously enough that everyone is still having fun.

SHELTER POINT BREAK**

5/6 oz (25 ml) single malt whisky
(Shelter Point Single Malt)
5/6 oz (25 ml) Shelter Point
Sunshine Liqueur
5/6 oz (25 ml) Lillet Blanc
5/6 oz (25 ml) Orange-aloe cordial
(p. 201)

Glass: Large Cocktail
Method: Shake all ingredients with
ice and double strain
Garnish: Flamed orange peel

SCOTT LANDSDOWNE

Born in Williams Lake, BC, on the day the Def Leppard drummer lost his left arm, Scott was raised in Kelowna. His only ambition growing up was to become incredibly rich, but that changed after his first experience with booze: Creating homemade absinthe with his beatnik friends to celebrate his eighteenth birthday. Residue from the noxious liquid quickly stained a permanent green ring onto the laminate countertop where it sat, and Scott knew he had found a very special passion.

He had a chance to put this passion into practice in 2012 when Cenote Restaurant opened. Most of Scott's duties with the fledgling restaurant involved managing the official Cenote foosball team. Soon, however, he dropped out of grad school to focus on learning to bartend and help develop Cenote's inimitable urban space. After seven years slinging drinks, Scott remains as passionate as ever.

RUM-A RUM-A DING DONG**

2 oz (60 ml) Gosling's Black Seal
¼ oz (7.5 ml) Campari
¼ oz (7.5 ml) pastis (Pernod)
1 oz (30 ml) Espresso syrup (p. 195)
¼ oz (7.5 ml) lime juice
6-8 mint leaves

Glass: Large Cocktail
Method: Shake all ingredients
with ice and double strain
Garnish: Orange twist

IN FOCUS

NATE CAUDLE & KYLE GUILFOYLE
NIMBLE BAR COMPANY

Nimble Bar Company is a bartender consultancy and the brainchild of Nate Caudle and Kyle Guilfoyle. Both have been driving forces behind Victoria's cocktail culture for many years, spearheading Little Jumbo's success from the beginning. Nate used to say, "I'm the only guy I know who'll still be bartending when I'm 60!" While he's shifted his career somewhat, he is still absolutely dedicated to helping bars and bartenders everywhere.

Kyle still loves the craft of cocktails, but he's shifted his focus to brand and marketing strategy. He now dedicates his time to helping companies identify their goals and designing campaigns. With these backgrounds, Nate and Kyle are a formidable duo that have been showcased in publications across Canada and the United States. Nimble Bar Company offers training, consultation, branding and marketing to the hospitality industry in Victoria and British Columbia.

SPURS & SADDLES*** BY NATE CAUDLE

1 ½ oz (45 ml) bourbon (Bulleit)
½ oz (15 ml) orange liqueur (Cointreau)
½ oz (15 ml) Root beer syrup (p. 204)
¾ oz (22.5 ml) lime juice

Glass: Old-Fashioned / Rocks
Method: Smoke glass on Nimble Smoking Puck, shake with ice and double strain into glass
Garnish: None

THE WHOLE SPECTRUM* BY KYLE GUILFOYLE

1 oz (30 ml) Cynar
1 oz (30 ml) Campari
½ oz (15 ml) Islay whisky (McClelland's)
¼ oz (7.5 ml) lemon juice
4 dashes Fee Brothers Peach Bitters
Pinch of salt

Glass: Old-Fashioned / Rocks
Method: Stir and strain onto king cube
Garnish: Lemon twist

JAYCE NOALS

During his 15 years working in many areas of the hospitality profession Jayce always held on to a casual side job as a bartender. A move to Victoria in 2013 brought a career shift when Jayce took on the manager/head bartender position at Clive's Classic Lounge—this challenge allowed him to make his hobby become his profession. In pursuit of progressing as a professional bartender Jayce has always placed value in the concept that you must love what you do. Jayce is at his best when behind the bar engaging with guests and providing unique experiences. His approach to creating cocktails focuses on flavor and balance, often incorporating a food element in his signature drinks. The cocktail program Jayce oversees at Clive's allows the bar team opportunity to be creative and think outside the bottle. When at work creating new cocktails, Jayce frequently finds inspiration by incorporating unusual spirits, liqueurs, food, seasonally harvested local products, and spice in his drinks.

RISE & SHINE**

1 ½ oz (45 ml) Espadin mezcal
(Los Siete Misterios Doba-Yej)
½ oz (15 ml) Cointreau
¾ oz (22.5 ml) lemon juice
½ oz (15 ml) grapefruit juice
½ oz (15 ml) Jalapeno syrup
(p. 198)
1 barspoon fresh avocado
1 egg white
1 dash Scrappy's Firewater Bitters
Pinch sal de chapulin spice (*sea salt, grasshopper and hot pepper spice mix*)

Glass: Old-Fashioned / Rocks
Method: Combine all ingredients, dry shake then wet shake, double strain into chilled glass
Garnish: Lightly dusted with sal de chapulin

BRANT PORTER

Brant started his career at the tender age of 11 at the family's Thai restaurant. Falling in love with the restaurant industry, Brant bussed tables and washed dishes until he was old enough to jump behind the bar. This is where he found his real passion. He began to read, research and geek out at bars, learning everything he could until he began working at Little Jumbo, his first true cocktail bar.

Brant stayed on there for a few years, honing his craft under the tutelage of Nate Caudle and Kyle Guilfoyle until being given the opportunity to take the helm of his own program at Prima Strada, a high-end Neapolitan pizzeria. Brant's thirst for evolution and progression ended up with him running the bar program at Little Jumbo alongside Avi Kunen, and eventually landing the role of bar manager at the newly renovated Veneto. As a young 25-year-old bartender he now leads a team, pushing the envelope of cocktail culture in Victoria at one of its original, premier cocktail bars.

HOTEL RIALTO**

2 oz (60 ml) Tanqueray Rangpur
3/4 oz (22.5 ml) fresh lemon juice
1/2 oz (15 ml) orgeat (Giffard)
1 dash Herbsaint
Egg white

Glass: Old-Fashioned / Rocks
Method: Dry shake then wet shake with ice and double strain into the glass over 3 inch by inch Cucumber ice cubes (p. 194)
Garnish: Mint sprig

STEPHEN QUIGLEY

Born and raised in Dublin, Ireland, Quigley started his career in the industry bussing tables and sweeping floors at the tender age of 12. At 17 he started as an apprentice cook and stayed in the back of house for the next 14 years, working in Ireland, Scotland, the Channel Islands and Australia before finally ending up in Paris in 2001, which is where he began his bartending career.

Stephen eventually moved to Victoria in 2007, where he helped open Stage Wine Bar to rave reviews. Stephen's style has always been curious and playful, with hospitality and banter coming second to playing with cocktails, infusions, and syrups. Stephen opened his own place in 2018 when he took over and revamped the popular Chorizo & Co. where he works the bar and can continue his love of the industry.

LAS RAMBLAS*

2 oz (60 ml) Spanish brandy (Fundador)
¼ oz (7.5 ml) Averna Amaro
¼ oz (7.5 ml) sweet vermouth (Noilly Prat Rouge)

Glass: Large Cocktail
Method: Stir all ingredients with ice and strain
Garnish: Orange twist

TIM SIEBERT

As the bar manager at Northern Quarter restaurant, Tim's philosophy towards bartending is to represent a sense of place: Terroir is not just for wine, it's applicable to everything he does at the venue. Northern Quarter is farm to table, so naturally he also focuses on seasonal ingredients and local producers. Tim runs a craft-focused bar, with strictly BC-grown and -produced beer, wine, and cider, plus a BC-first focus on distilled products.

Tim's drinks are designed to be approachable and easily reproduced. He is very particular when choosing his ingredients, as he is looking to build complex flavours with minimal ingredients. His mentality is not trying to reinvent the wheel, he just wants to make sure everyone's having a good time while he keeps it spinning.

ODDY TODDY**

1 ½ oz (45 ml) single malt whisky (DeVine Ancient Grains)
¼ oz (7.5 ml) nocino (Ampersand)
½ oz (15 ml) Honey chai syrup (p. 197)
¼ oz (7.5 ml) lemon juice

Glass: Large Cocktail
Method: Shake with ice and double strain
Garnish: Lemon twist

SOLOMON SIEGEL

Solomon was born and raised in the Victoria restaurant world. He started bartending before he should have at his family's joint, Pagliacci's; he has now been bartending for 17 years. Solomon operated his eponymous establishment for 18 months, where Victoria's cocktail scene got its much-needed start. Solomon's was ahead of its time, emulating the cutting-edge cocktail culture of New York and San Francisco; it was immediately popular with a niche audience of locals that craved that cultural exposure.

Solomon is now "back home" as the general manager of Pagliacci's. His proudest achievement is all the young local bartenders that have worked for him and gone on to their own greatness.

THE REBUJITO QUIXOTIC* / ***

2 oz (60 ml) manzanilla sherry (Hidalgo La Gitana)
½ oz (15 ml) Simple syrup (p. 209)
½ oz (15 ml) lemon juice
2 ½ oz (75 ml) water or soda (simple method)

Glass: Tasting Glass / ISO
Methods: (*Simple*) Shake all ingredients with ice except soda, double strain neat and top with soda; (*Difficult*) Shake all ingredients in a Perlini carbonation shaker with ice and strain neat
Garnish: Mint sprig wrapped in lemon twist

ALEX SNOW

Alex describes himself of a cocktail enthusiast come cocktail bartender. Self-taught, he dedicated endless hours to researching recipes, menus, and techniques online, in vintage books, and sitting perched on bar stools, where he studied the bartender's movements involved in executing the proper delivery of a quality drink. He challenges himself by crafting original bitters, tinctures and syrups—everything from a dill tincture, or turmeric and cinnamon spritz, to charred fenugreek and masala simple syrup.

The greatest pleasure he derives from this passion is combining it with his other love—literature. He has compiled successful menus, each relating to a classic work of literature, each with a complex story to tell about the ingredients of the drink.

LES FLEURS DU MAL***

1 oz (30 ml) gin (Odd Society Wallflower Gin)
½ oz (15 ml) creme de violette
¼ oz (7.5 ml) ginger liqueur (Bols)
¼ oz (7.5 ml) lychee liqueur (Soho)
3 dashes rose water
½ oz (15 ml) lemon juice

Glass: Large Cocktail
Method: Stir all ingredients with ice and double strain into a glass that's been spritzed with Lavender tincture (p. 199)
Garnish: Dried hibiscus flowers

JHOL SPINDLER

Jhol Spindler hasn't been bartending for all that long, but with some great mentorship by some of Victoria's finest bartenders, and a strong work ethic, he's quickly managed to familiarize himself to those in the Victoria cocktail scene. Jhol wasn't sure where he was going when he gave up his construction job to join the hospitality industry. That is, until he was fortunate enough to gain employment at his first cocktail bar, The Guild Freehouse, where he began his training under the tutelage of Shawn Soole.

Since then, Jhol followed Shawn to reopen Café Mexico, a place that has been an institution in Victoria for over 30 years, eventually taking his place as general manager. Jhol has now set out to make it the go-to Mexican restaurant to a more authentic place, one that presently boasts more than 120 different agave spirits, one of the largest collections of such in all of Canada.

WATERMELON GIN SMASH**

2oz (60 ml) gin (Beefeater)
1oz (30 ml) Watermelon syrup (p. 209)
¾ oz (22.5 ml) lemon juice
8-10 mint leaves
Top with Soda

Glass: Highball / Collins
Method: Shake all ingredients with ice and double strain over fresh ice
Garnish: Watermelon wedge and mint sprig

VINCENT VANDERHEIDE

Vincent had always aspired to be a bartender. He began his career as a busser at Canoe, a massive brewery restaurant on the harbor in Victoria. He worked hard and finally got his shot at a spot behind the wood, where he held a six-year tenure. He left to explore a career at the recently renovated Fairmont Empress Q Bar, working with state-of-the-art equipment and serving the rich and famous that make their way through the halls of the Victoria icon.

After a few years at the Q Bar, he was enticed back to Canoe with its spectacular patio during summer, the cold, in-house brewed craft beer pouring, and live music. He is now the bar manager and is currently in the process of blending the beauty that is craft beer and cocktails into the menu. His new drinks list will be beer focused and he couldn't be more excited about it.

BETTER BELIEVE THAT'S A'PADDLIN'**

1 oz (30ml) Charred pineapple, allspice and clove-infused añejo rum (Havana Club) (p. 192)
1 oz (30 ml) orange juice
½ oz (15 ml) lemon juice
¼ oz (7.5 ml) passion fruit purée
3 oz (90 ml) Belgian-style witbier

Glass: Highball / Collins
Method: Combine all ingredients except for witbier in shaker. Shake with ice and strain over fresh ice. Top with witbier
Garnish: Spritz of crème de violette and an orange twist

DUNCAN

SITUATED on the long road up island, Duncan has become a hub for the Comox Valley and the many people who live there but still work the hour-plus drive south in Victoria. As a result of this, a smart culture of little bistros and bars serving quality products that are on par with the restaurants in Victoria has sprung up, with Old Firehouse becoming a beacon in Duncan's foodie scene that has completely reinvented the way people dine in Duncan.

IN FOCUS

JEFF DOWNIE
Old Firehouse Wine & Cocktail Bar

Jeff's affection for the hospitality industry began in 1984 at the age of 14 while working at Lower Mainland classic the Park Royal Hotel in West Vancouver. He bussed tables and mimicked, as best he could, the mannerisms and serving styles and affectations of the dynamic professional wait staff. The Clyde Dining Room at the Park was a bastion of wine and food culture in the area and there was so much to learn.

By the time Jeff had turned 19, he was a bartender and wine steward and was taken under the wing of several of the pros. Jeff found the bartenders to be rock stars and he wanted every part of this lifestyle and discipline. In 1992 Jeff left the Lower Mainland for the Cowichan Valley on Vancouver Island.

He worked for three-plus years as a fine-dining server in Duncan's Hy's Steakhouse. In 1996 Jeff left his beloved industry, having faced substance addictions and sought complete sobriety. He, with the help of his parents, sought entrepreneurialism and bought a small business in the shape of a used and rare bookshop.

By 2011, Jeff felt he needed a dramatic change and he and his wife Alanah built the Old Firehouse Wine and Cocktail Bar in the space where they owned the shop. Jeff has come to terms with his sobriety and has returned to his true passion of hospitality and bartending. Jeff feels he has the nose of a greyhound and the passion and fear of an honest craftsman. He enjoys making drinks immensely and seeks balance in his business, his life and the cocktails he creates. Known as the Wine Bar in Duncan, they are in their eighth year and look forward to the beautiful revolution of craftsmanship on Vancouver Island continuing to blossom for many years to come.

NOURISHING PASSION**

1 ¼ oz (37.5 ml) London dry gin (Ampersand Distilling)
¼ oz (7.5 ml) Green Chartreuse
¾ oz (22.5 ml) Lavender syrup (p. 199)
2 dashes Victoria Spirits Black Pepper Bitters
1 oz (30 ml) lemon juice

Glass: Large
Cocktail
Method: Muddle
fresh mint then
shake with ice
and double strain
Garnish: Fresh
rose petal

TOFINO

ON THE FAR EAST coast of Vancouver Island is the seaside surf town of Tofino. Long held as the escape on the island for surfers and storm watchers alike, it has also become home to some of the best food and drink in the country. Hyper-seasonality has created a microcosm of world-class chefs and bartenders who serve the throngs of tourists that visit the town every summer, getting away from the bustle of the big cities without sacrificing the culinary excellence to which they are accustomed.

IN FOCUS

HAILEY PASEMKO & KEN GIFFORD
WOLF IN THE FOG

Ken and Hailey each spent many years developing their bartending careers before working together at Wolf in the Fog. They were both drawn to Tofino at different times by the natural beauty and coastal lifestyle. Fortunately, they were able to find their professional homes behind the bar there as well. They now run the bar program inspired by the local bounty that Tofino has to offer. They create unique cocktails featuring many house-made products, foraged ingredients, and local spirits, providing a cocktail experience unlike anywhere else on Vancouver Island.

CEDAR SOUR** BY HAILEY PASEMKO

2 oz (60 ml) Cedar rye (p. 191)
¾ oz (22.5 ml) Lemon thyme syrup (p. 199)
1 oz (30 ml) lemon juice
1oz (30 ml) egg white

Glass: Old-Fashioned / Rocks
Method: Dry shake all ingredients then shake with ice and double strain
Garnish: Three cherries

HIGH FIVES AND

BELLY RIDES** BY KEN GIFFORD

1 ¾ oz (52.5 ml) gin (Sheringham Gin)
½ oz (15 ml) apricot brandy (Giffard)
½ oz (15 ml) Geisha syrup (p. 195)
1 oz (30 ml) lime juice
2 slices of cucumber muddled
1-2 oz (30-60 ml) sparkling wine (Bella Blanc de Blanc)

Glass: Large Cocktail
Method: Shake everything except sparkling wine with ice and double strain. Top with sparkling wine
Garnish: Cucumber slice

52

VANCOUVER

VANCOUVER is the metropolis of British Columbia. Weirdly enough it's not the capital of the province, but it's definitely the biggest city. I once heard a story that when they were deciding on what the capital of the province was going to be, the delegates from Vancouver came to Victoria for the vote. The night before the vote, the Victorian contingent took the Vancouver party out for a night on the town. Needless to say, the Victorians drank the Vancouverites under the table and only half of the visiting party showed up to vote on the capital the next day. Regardless If the story is true or not, it's a great one.

Vancouver is an atypical big city, with mountains to the north and ocean to the south; and neighbourhoods of bars and restaurants all catering to a different clientele. It's the hub for the west coast of Canada, and a city that showcases the melting pot that is the Pacific Northwest, with its Asian fusion, Indian influences, and everything in between. This diversity in flavors and styles is evident in its cocktail culture, which is an incubator that allows bartenders from the world over to share knowledge and experiences with each other, creating one of the world's best scenes.

IN FOCUS

LAUREN MOTE
& JONATHON CHOVANCEK
BITTERED SLING

Bittered Sling Bitters celebrates the unique life and business partnership of celebrated chef Jonathan Chovancek and award-winning mixologist/ sommelier Lauren Mote, who together have contributed more than 30 years of professional experience, knowledge, and innovation to the Canadian food and beverage industry. Mote has been making bitters since 2008 — over half her career. The sweetest partnership launched on February 12, 2012, when Mote and Chovancek unveiled their Bittered Sling line up to the world: A retail line of high-quality cocktail bitters, and culinary extracts that use exceptional ingredients, providing the palate, plate, and potion with powerful and exciting fusions of flavors. The brand quickly built a reputation in the international cocktail and culinary community as a premium, high-quality cocktail bitters, celebrating stories of travel and terroir, utilizing the finest quality ingredients.

A mixologist; a sommelier; an architect of potions, tonics and elixirs; an accomplished emcee, writer, spirit, and cocktail judge; an international spirits diplomat and accredited instructor; award-winning bartender Lauren Mote wears many hats, but she's perhaps best known as the Diageo Reserve & World Class Global Cocktailian. Named the 2015 Bartender of the Year by both the Vancouver Magazine Restaurant Awards and Diageo World Class Canada, Lauren is a well-respected speaker, educator, mentor, and industry advocate, whose reach extends well beyond the bar. She has served as an associate director for the CPBA (Canadian Professional Bartenders Association), has been an event partner, and keynote speaker with Tales of the Cocktail since 2011, and in 2016 Lauren was the first Canadian woman inducted into the Dames Hall of Fame, and nominated for Best Bar Mentor at the 10th annual Spirited Awards.

Lauren is an in-demand hospitality consultant and in the past five years has launched and redesigned bar programs at The Nash Restaurant & Off Cut Bar

54

in Calgary; Vancouver's Café Medina and Burdock & Co.; and most recently collaborated as the beverage consultant for the Four Seasons Hotel Vancouver and its restaurant, YEW seafood + bar.

For more than 25 years, chef Jonathan Chovancek's abundant enthusiasm, inspired creativity and commitment to healthy eating has provided a winning recipe for some of British Columbia's most celebrated restaurants. A firm believer in the Slow Food movement, Chovancek's culinary philosophy of sourcing the best fresh, local and sustainable ingredients has driven his menus from the time he anchored back-of-house teams at Vancouver Island's Relais & Chateaux property The Aerie Resort, Sooke Harbour House, and Zambri's as well as Culinary Capers in Vancouver. He has cooked in China, Mexico, Italy, the United States, and Canada as well as consults on culinary programming and menu development throughout North America.

Jonathan, who was the chef/host of CBC TV's ground-breaking documentary *Village on a Diet* in 2011, is also an in-demand speaker, as well as a dedicated coach and mentor to up-and-coming kitchen talent. Chovancek was also most recently the executive chef for Wentworth Hospitality Group, including iconic Vancouver restaurants Homer Street Cafe & Bar and Tableau Bistro.

THE CHARTREUSE MILKSHAKE*

1 ½ oz (45 ml) London dry gin (Tanqueray No. Ten)
½ oz (15 ml) white crème de cacao
½ oz (15 ml) Green Chartreuse
½ oz (15 ml) orange juice
½ oz (15 ml) lime juice
¾ oz (22.5 ml) Simple syrup (p.209)
2 dashes Bittered Sling Malagasy Chocolate Bitters
1 egg white

Glass: Highball / Collins
Method: Shake with ice and double strain over fresh ice
Garnish: Fresh shavings of raw cacao bean

ALEX BLACK

Alex has spent over 15 years in the hospitality industry. He started his career in Winnipeg where he cut his teeth in all sorts of establishments from concert venues, casual restaurants, pool halls, nightclubs, and even a karaoke bar. After a brief long-distance love affair with Vancouver, he packed his bags and moved there on New Year's Day in 2011 to ply his trade in its world-class bar and hospitality community at many of Vancouver's top-tier restaurants and bars, including establishments under the umbrellas of the Donnelly Group, Glowbal Restaurant Group and Hawksworth Restaurant Group.

Alex has gained a number of qualifications, including the BarSmarts Advanced and International Sommeliers Guild Level 1and the West Indies Rum and Spirit Producers Association's ACR Diploma). He became one of the first people in the world to achieve the Level 3 Diploma in Spirits from the Wine & Spirit Education Trust (WSET).

THE ANCIENT RUIN*

1 ½ oz (45 ml) Serrano-infused mezcal (Los Siete Misterios Espadin) (p. 206)
½ oz (15 ml) white crème de cacao
¾ oz (22.5 ml) lemon juice
½ oz (15 ml) agave syrup

Glass: Large Cocktail
Method: Shake all ingredients with ice and double strain
Garnish: Freshly grated tonka bean

MAX BORROWMAN

Max started bartending in 2006 when he took up shop at Earls, a high-volume, rooftop patio bar in Kelowna. Later moving to Victoria, Max tailored his fine-dining skills at the Marina Restaurant in Oak Bay. He then moved to Vancouver in 2010 where he started learning the art of cocktails from Jacob Sweetapple and Grant Sceney at the Fairmont Pacific Rim. The Lobby Lounge was his home for several years until summer 2015 when he took on his first bar manager role at Torafuku in Chinatown. Max has been competing at a high level since, travelling to Toronto and Washington DC for national cocktail competitions for various brands.

In 2016 Max found his home as bar manager at Juniper Kitchen Bar. Juniper has since been ranked in the top 80 best gin bars in the world. Max's cocktail program at Juniper is ever evolving as he continues to learn and grow. His main source of inspiration is his extensive travels abroad, having been to Oaxaca, New York City, all over Europe and Africa, South America, as well as Australia and Southeast Asia.

FLATIRON NEGRONI*

1 oz (30 ml) gin (Monkey 47)
1 ¼ oz (37.5 ml) sweet vermouth
(Carpano Antica Formula)
¾ oz (22.5 ml) Campari
¼ oz (7.5 ml) fresh espresso
2 dashes Apothecary Darkness
Bitters

Glass: Old-Fashioned / Rocks
Method: Stir all ingredients with ice and strain over large ice chunk
Garnish: Lemon peel

CAM BROWN

Born and raised in British Columbia, Cameron Brown started his bartending career in Kelowna and has spent the past 10 years moving back and forth between the Okanagan and Vancouver, running many bar programs along the way. He has worked in every aspect of this industry—from nightclubs to pubs, fine-dining restaurants, and in cocktail bars. During this time, he has also spent months on the road doing guest shifts at top bars and traveling the world.

Cam is extremely passionate about both the local and global bartending communities, lending his time on the board of directors for the CPBA and spending three years as a part of the Cocktail Apprenticeship Program at Tales of the Cocktail in New Orleans. Always fascinated by spirits, cocktails and the history of the industry, in 2019 he also completed the BAR 5-Day program in New York. Cam is currently the head bartender at Clough Club in Vancouver.

LIKE FATHER, LIKE SON*

1 ½ oz (45 ml) American rye (Rittenhouse)
½ oz (15 ml) dry vermouth
¼ oz (7.5 ml) maraschino (Luxardo)
½ oz (15 ml) Campari
½ oz (15 ml) amaro (Legend Distilling Naramaro)

Glass: Small Cocktail / Nick & Nora
Method: Stir all ingredients with a lemon peel in the mixing glass over ice, strain neat
Garnish: none

AMBER BRUCE

Amber Bruce, bar manager of the Keefer Bar in Vancouver's Chinatown, has over 10 years of experience behind bars designing unique cocktails. She has worked alongside some of Vancouver's best bartenders and has travelled around the world, visiting distilleries as well as hosting guest shifts and pop-up bars. She has collected a few awards and accolades, including Speed Rack National Finalist 2019, Best Bartender by the Georgia Straight 2018, Giffard Iron Mixologist 2017, Diageo World Class National Finalist 2016 and 2017, and winner of the Absolut Bartending Competition.

In addition to working behind the bar, Amber volunteers on the board of the CPBA as the vice president, helping to grow and connect the community of British Columbia bartenders. She is also a founding member of MiniBar Canada, a social enterprise celebrating and promoting women in the restaurant and beverage industry.

QUIXOTE'S FOLLY**

1 ¼ oz (37.5 ml) añejo tequila (Don Julio Añejo)
¾ oz (22.5 ml) genever (Bols)
½ oz (15 ml) Chamomile maple syrup (p. 191)
¾ oz (22.5 ml) lemon juice

Glass: Large Cocktail
Method: Shake all ingredients with ice and double strain
Garnish: Chamomile flower and dried lemon wheel

AIMEE CORNO

Corno was raised on a ranch outside of a small town, in the forest; a hands-on nature experience where her family did everything, including trimming and butchering their own meat. Mimicking her mother's talents in the kitchen for flavor and creation she became enthralled with cooking and joined a kitchen as an apprentice at 14. Turning 18 while attending university she tried her hand at working front of house, serving and growing into a bartender position at a Calgary pub.

A chef friend asked for her help to create a cocktail program for his new bistro; this was the spark that started her researching the classics, experimenting with flavors, and launching an honest classics list for him two months later. With the fire lit, she made the move to Vancouver to build on her passion and after a tough year of grinding out unfulfilling jobs, she got a spot at Homer St. Café, with J.S. Dupuis managing the bar. Under the tutelage of J.S., Aimee had a crash course in flavors, participated in her first competition, and eventually took her first bar managing position at Acorn. Since then, she has been exploring her creativity in the bars she manages, most especially at her current space at the Waldorf Hotel, in a classic tiki bar that she has helped reinvent.

CHASE THE RABBIT *

1 oz (30 ml) Canadian whisky (Forty Creek Double Barrel)
¾ oz (22.5 ml) amaretto (Sons of Vancouver)
½ oz (15 ml) fino sherry (Alvear Single Varietal)
2 oz (60 ml) Rabbit chaser syrup (p. 203)
¾ oz (22.5 ml) egg white
½ oz (15 ml) lime juice
½ oz (15 ml) lemon juice
1 dash aromatic bitters

Glass: Large Cocktail
Method: Shake all ingredients with ice and double strain
Garnish: Salted maple tuile

MAX CURZON-PRICE

Max is one of Vancouver's imports from across the sea—from Brighton, England. Classically trained in hotel bars, his love for the world of sugar cane and the tiki movement brought him to run a handful of small bars in the lanes of Brighton. Tired of the pretentious and relatively stuffy cocktail scene, Max decided to bring a little jazz and flair to it with a modern interpretation of classic tiki culture. "Once you remove the fun from drinking, you've really lost the point", a phrase he often repeated to remind himself to keep both service and drinks fun, pun-driven and perhaps a little eclectic. Now based out of Vancouver, Max works at Botanist at the Fairmont Pacific Rim. The drinks continue to be playful with a sense of sophistication and a hint of whimsy.

John Cynar is one of his signature serves. "I enjoy bombastic, rich flavours. I like looking for a sense of umami or salinity in a cocktail and I really appreciate a balance where you start to see flavour profiles move out of the usual sweet/sour/bitter balance," he explains. "I also appreciate that on a night out, sometimes it's wise to take it a little slower and move into the more aperitif/digestif-driven, low-ABV direction. This drink is a homage to this idea, named appropriately after everyone's favourite house-hold wrestler John Cena."

JOHN CYNAR*

2 oz (60 ml) Cynar
½ oz (15 ml) apricot brandy (Giffard)
3 dashes absinthe
1 dash Angostura bitters
1 small pinch of salt
6-8 large, fresh mint leaves

Glass: Julep Mug
Method: Shake all ingredients with ice and strain over crushed ice
Garnish: Large sprig of mint and torched star anise

SABRINE DHALIWAL

Sabrine Dhaliwal, national ambassador for Belvedere Vodka and Hennessy cognac, is no stranger to the hospitality industry. Since moving to Vancouver in 2009, she has been continuously learning, reading, tasting and researching wine, beer and spirits. WSET accredited, Sabrine moved from the service floor to behind the bar in 2012; a few years later, she found herself on the global stage at the Belvedere Challenge representing Canada. After two days of fierce competition against bartenders from around the world, she proudly brought home the top prize. Sabrine has since led great cocktail programs at some of Vancouver's top restaurant and bars such as West Restaurant and Uva Wine & Cocktail Bar, the latter of which was named a Top 10 Restaurant Bar in the Americas by the Spirited Awards in 2018.

VOYAGER'S ESCAPE**

1 ½ oz (45 ml) Hennessy VSOP cognac
½ oz (15 ml) Pistachio and apricot orgeat (p. 203)
1/3 oz (10 ml) pineapple juice
2/3 oz (20 ml) lemon juice
½ oz (15 ml) banana liqueur
2 dashes Bittered Sling Plum & Rootbeer Bitters

Glass: Tiki Mug / Collins
Method: Shake all ingredients with ice and strain over crushed ice
Garnish: Pineapple leaves , cherry, and umbrella

ADAM DOMET

Whether it's his desire to master new tricks, a seemingly inexhaustible knowledge of spirits or near total recall of the smallest detail or preferred drink of a past guest's experience, there's no shortage of skills in Adam Domet's bartending arsenal. Originally from Toronto, Adam traded Hogtown for Vancouver following its Winter Olympics heyday in 2010 and got his first gig in the local hospitality scene at Gastown's The Diamond, where he worked in a variety of roles and quickly built his knowledge by learning from some of the city's best drink-slingers. In 2017, he became the latest friendly face to join the front-of-house family at Pourhouse.

His favorite aspect of holding court behind the pine at Pourhouse is the many regulars who challenge him and his staff to be the best they can be and encourage their creativity:

"We are fortunate to cater to a very savvy crowd with specific tastes and well-developed palates, many of whom have been coming to Pourhouse since it opened almost a decade ago—people have developed a real connection to this place and we're happy to welcome them home whenever they walk through the door."

BURNT GIBSON MARTINI*

2 oz (60 ml) London dry gin (Ford's)
½ oz (15 ml) dry vermouth (Madenii)
1/6 oz (5 ml) mezcal (Los Siete Misterios Doba Yej)

Glass: Small Cocktail / Nick & Nora
Method: Stir all ingredients with ice and strain
Garnish: Pickled pearl onion

CHRIS ENNS

Chris Enns began his bartending career over 10 years ago and hasn't looked back. Originally from Saskatoon, he spent the first five years learning the craft before moving to Vancouver in 2013. There, he worked at The Diamond before heading to the Fairmont Pacific Rim Hotel. Chris has also been active in a number of cocktail competitions. In 2016 Chris represented Vancouver in the Grey Goose Pour Masters, Bacardi Legacy, and Diageo World Class national finals. Two years later he was named the 2018 Woodford Reserve Master of the Manhattan as well the 2018 Diageo World Class Canadian Bartender of the Year.

STANLEY PARK**

1 ½ oz (45 ml) gin (Tanqueray No. Ten)
½ oz (15 ml) fino sherry (Tio Pepe)
¾ oz (22.5 ml) lime juice
¾ oz (22.5 ml) Chamomile syrup (p. 191)
1 dash absinthe
1 dash Scrappy's Cardamom Bitters

Glass: Large Cocktail
Method: Shake all ingredients with ice and double strain
Garnish: Sprig of thyme

ROBYN GRAY

Robyn Alexander Gray was born and raised in Canada's beautiful Vancouver, BC. Launching his career at age 18 in Glasgow, Scotland he has worked in many settings from restaurants to nightclubs, cocktail bars to hotel lounges while pursuing a true sense of hospitality.

Robyn has worked since 2011 in Vancouver's Rosewood Hotel Georgia. As hotel head bartender he has opened and operated all hotel lounges including Reflections: the Garden Terrace, 1927 Lobby Lounge, and the Prohibition Speakeasy. With over 400 seats and an award-winning cocktail program recognized by Canada's 50 Best Bars, Gray continues to create an atmosphere of luxury and allure sought by bon vivants alike. Winning cocktail competitions such as Grey Goose Pour Masters in 2014 and Bombay Sapphire's Mixology Challenge in 2010, he has since judged for competitions such as Bacardi Legacy and Patrón Perfectionists.

Attending bar shows from Lisbon to Athens and Edinburgh, as well as presenting at Tales of the Cocktail in New Orleans, and constantly imbibing new information allows him to stay on the forefront of his industry. As a holder of the CSS (Certified Specialist of Spirits) and secretary of the CPBA, Robyn finesses the bounds of his industry by putting hospitality first and creating engaging experience for his guests.

INCEPTION NEGRONI***

Preparation for Service: White Negroni
2/3 oz (20 ml) London dry gin
2/3 oz (20 ml) Luxardo Bitter Bianco
2/3 oz (20 ml) Martini Bianco

Glass: Old-Fashioned / Rocks
Method: Stir all ingredients with ice and strain over Negroni Ice Sphere (see below)
Garnish: Lemon twist

Negroni Ice Sphere Production
Using a Tovolo ice sphere mold, fill with water and freeze until the contents are partly frozen. Depending on the freezer's temperature the timing will be variable, but 3-5 hours should suffice. Part freezing

creates a shell of ice and a liquid water interior will remain. In the meantime, make the batch Negroni recipe below and place in freezer:

200 ml gin

200 ml Campari

200 ml sweet vermouth

Use a large syringe with a large needle to pierce the shell and extract water. Inject the frozen Negroni batch. Recap the hole by dripping cold water on it.

66

SHEA HOGAN

Shea Hogan was born in small town Chemainus on Vancouver Island, and now resides in beautiful Port Coquitlam. Following high school and a three-year hiatus in Canmore, Alberta, Shea returned to BC and took up automotive collision repair and is a fully red-seal certified technician. After 8 years or so he retired from that trade and took up a new career, becoming a bartender. In early 2013 Shea stumbled upon the tiki bartending lifestyle and was an opening bartender of the Shameful Tiki Room, where he quickly rose to the top and became bar manager. Since then he has dabbled with a brand ambassadorial role with Lemon Hart rum, before embarking on his own journey of starting his own business in 2018, PoCo Soap Co.

FOMO DAIQUIRI*

2 oz (60 ml) overproof rum
(Wray & Nephew)
¾ oz (22.5 ml) lime juice
¾ oz (22.5 ml) Coconut
syrup (p. 193)

Glass: Large Cocktail
Method: Shake all
ingredients with ice and
double strain
Garnish: Dehydrated lime
wheel

KATIE INGRAM

Over the past 10 years, Katie Ingram has devoted her energy, skill and creativity to the food and beverage industry. As a specialist in the cocktail and spirits world, Katie provides her work with a level of grace and hospitality that has helped propel her to the top of the industry. Her past endeavors as the lead bartender at downtown Vancouver's UVA Wine & Cocktail Bar, and bar manager at both L'Abattoir, and its sister restaurant Coquille Fine Seafood has helped pave the way for countless competition wins, educational trips, and now her role as the bar manager at Elisa Wood-Fired Grill.

In addition to her role at Elisa, Katie is one of the Canadian Ambassadors for Bittered Sling. She competes in cocktail competitions and was a Top 4 National Finalist for Diageo's World Class Canada in 2018 and 2019. With her additional fluency in French, a flair for romantic languages, and background in vocal and performing arts, Katie adds a certain spice and talent to everything she does both personally and professionally.

PEACH DON'T KILL MY VIBE*

1 ½ oz (45 ml) blanco tequila (Don Julio)
½ oz (15 ml) apricot brandy (Giffard)
½ oz (15 ml) blue curaçao (Sons of Vancouver)
2/3 oz (20 ml) lime juice
1/3 oz (10 ml) Simple syrup (p. 209)
2 dashes Bittered Sling Clingstone Peach

Glass: Large Cocktail
Method: Shake all ingredients with ice and double strain
Garnish: Dehydrated lime wheel and/or dehydrated rose bud

68

PHILIPP KARATSYUPA

That Russian fella with an unpronounceable last name, taking over the west coast of Canada one bar at the time, started his spiritual journey back in 2001 when his mom opened her first restaurant downtown in Moscow and was the first to legalize and bring absinthe into Russia.

Philipp moved to Vancouver in 2010 and got hired a few years later by the Donnelly Group at New Oxford where he started making cocktails under the strict supervision of Trevor Kallies. Philipp has studied and received several credentials including most recently the CSS. After two-and-a-half years at the helm of the bar program at Ancora Waterfront Dining and Patio and making hundreds of Pisco Sours per weekend, he has now moved on to become the bar manager at the award winning L'Abattoir.

MY MEZCAL MARTINEZ*

1 ½ oz (45 ml) mezcal (Mezcal Cuishe)
½ oz (15 ml) Luxardo Abano Amaro
¼ oz (7.5 ml) maraschino (Luxardo)
2 dashes Ms. Better's Chocolate Bitters

Glass: Small Cocktail / Nick & Nora
Method: Stir all ingredients with ice and strain
Garnish: Orange twist

SHAUN LAYTON

Shaun Layton is a born and raised Vancouverite with over 15 years of experience in the local restaurant industry. As owner of Como Taperia, Shaun has opened his dream bar—a new Barcelona/Madrid-style tapas bar in Mt. Pleasant. He's managed bar programs at places such as George, L'Abattoir, and Juniper in the immediate past, and has been running a consulting business for the last few years, working with venues including Coquille, Boulevard, Hook, Espana, The Distillery Bar, Earl's, and Miku/Minami. He has many accolades to his name: Vancouver Bartender of the Year for *Vancouver Magazine*; reviews in *Western Living*, *Georgia Straight*, and *W.E.*; and named in *Western Living*'s Top 40 under 40. Shaun also writes a column about the beverage industry for *Scout Magazine*, BC's leading food and beverage publication.

SL NEGRONI*

1 oz (30 ml) Northwest gin
(Aviation gin)
1 oz (30 ml) El Bandarra
Vermut
½ oz (15 ml) Campari
1/3 oz (10 ml) Aperol
1/3 oz (10 ml) fino sherry

Glass: Old-Fashioned /
Rocks
Method: Stir over ice in
glass
Garnish: Sangria-infused
grapefruit slice

SEAN MCGUIGAN

Hailing from North Vancouver, Sean discovered his passion for spirits and cocktails while working at a pub in Vancouver's Gastown district, the city's hub of cocktail culture in the late 2000s. Inspired by the drinks being made at The Keefer and The Diamond, the first of the new wave of modern cocktail bars established in Vancouver, he sought an opportunity to make proper cocktails.

This came in 2013, when he landed a bartending position at Clough Club in Gastown, where he benefitted early on from the mentorship of Jay Jones, one of Canada's best-known cocktail innovators. Since then, Sean has competed in several major cocktail competitions including the Canadian Finals of Diageo World Class 2018, the North American finals of the 2018 Diplomático World Tournament, and the Canadian finals of Bacardi Legacy 2017.

In 2016, Sean joined the team at the Lobby Lounge at the Fairmont Pacific Rim Hotel, a luxury nightlife destination that is also one of Vancouver's foremost sushi restaurants. He was promoted to head bartender in 2017 and has since led the development of the Lobby Lounge's seasonal cocktail program, drawing inspiration from Japanese culture and ingredients.

Sean has a deep passion for spirits, particularly rum, whiskey, and amaro. His infatuation for the latter recently earned him a trip to Italy to participate in the second iteration of Amari Club, which brought together a group of bartenders from around the world to visit the homes of Averna, Braulio, and Cynar.

SHOGUN**

2 oz (60 ml) Japanese whisky (Nikka Coffey Malt Whisky)
½ oz (15 ml) madeira (Blandy's 5-year Malmsey)
½ oz (15 ml) Coffee bean-infused Cynar (p. 193)
¼ oz (7.5 ml) Spiced raisin cordial (p. 207)

Glass: Old-Fashioned / Rocks
Method: Stir with ice and strain over large ice cube
Garnish: Star anise pod atop a dehydrated lemon wheel

TARQUIN MELNYK

Since 2010, Tarquin Melnyk has been an awarded bartender in numerous cities globally. After transitioning from a career in health care, Tarquin set out on a quest to elevate beverage culture and provide a lasting experience for everyone he serves.

He resettled in 2014 on Canada's west coast and took over the bar at Bambudda in Vancouver's Gastown, where he transformed it into one of the city's most notable and adventurous cocktail bars. Tarquin's love for innovative molecular drinks led him to an involvement with Ms. Better's Bitters, a line of high-quality bitters, syrups, purées, and its innovative Vegan Miraculous Foamer.

Tarquin is a member of the team at Long Table Distillery as brand ambassador and distillery bartender, overseeing its rise in respect and global availability. In addition, he is a prolific writer, photographer, consultant, and filmmaker, hosting globally-recognized content on a number of sites, including his own, called *Project Happy Days*.

THE JOYCE*

1 ¾ oz (52.5 ml) London dry gin (Long Table)
1 oz (30 ml) fresh lemon
2/3 oz (20 ml) rhubarb syrup (Ms. Better's)
2 dashes Ms. Better's Green Strawberry Mah Kwan Bitters

Glass: Large Cocktail
Method: Shake all ingredients with ice and double strain
Garnish: Dehydrated strawberry slice

RON OLIVER

One of the original "old dogs" on Vancouver's cocktail scene with 22 years in the industry, Oliver has worked everywhere from Match Bar in London to Greece and all the way to Sydney, Australia. He settled in Vancouver in 2003 and began his illustrious tenure in the city's cocktail scene. He's worked at dives and high-end bars, been a brand ambassador for a stint, and finally opened his own place in 2013—Mamie Taylor's—where he still works the wood on a weekly basis. He's a definitive bartender who is all about the conversation, classic cocktails, and not talking about the ice programme.

DETROIT ROCK CITY*

1 oz (30 ml) bourbon (Maker's Mark)
1/3 oz (10 ml) Cynar
1/3 oz (10 ml) Lillet Blanc
1/3 oz (10 ml) Ramazzotti
1 dash Angostura Aromatic bitters
1 dash Angostura Orange bitters

Glass: Old-Fashioned / Rocks
Method: Stir all ingredients with ice and strain over fresh ice
Garnish: Orange twist

JEFF SAVAGE

Born in the Foothills, Jeff Savage has lived in a multitude of cities and worked in several different fields. After finishing his degrees in Turkey, Jeff found himself working for the University of Alberta, creating what would become the Office of Sustainability. Though he found his work meaningful and engaging, Jeff desired a more creative and hands-on career, which led him to bartending. After being on the opening team at Three Boars, Jeff worked at Tavern 1903, Woodwork, and eventually moved on to open the award-winning Proof Cocktail Bar. He is currently leading the cocktail program at Botanist in the Fairmont Pacific Rim in Vancouver.

Jeff is perpetually excited about the history of the cocktail world and is eager to contribute to its future. He believes that there are amazing flavours, textures, and combinations rooted in history and in nature that are still waiting to be rediscovered. While working in Botanist, Jeff aims to showcase the natural bounty of the world, while respectfully incorporating tradition and culture into his bartending practice and also elevating the conversation about the hospitality industry in Canada.

EL SANTO***

1 ½ oz (45 ml) mezcal (Los Misterios Doba-Yej)
¾ oz (22.5 ml) Amaro Montenegro
¼ oz (7.5 ml) white crème de cacao
1 barspoon agave nectar

Glass: Old-Fashioned / Rocks
Method: Flame a piece of Palo Santo wood until burning. Cover with a rocks glass and allow to fill with smoke. Stir all ingredients with ice and strain into sidecar / carafe. When serving, upend smoked glass and pour cocktail into glass
Garnish: None

GRANT SCENEY

Grant Sceney oversees the cocktail program for the Fairmont Pacific Rim and can be found shaking cocktails behind the bar at the Lobby Lounge, as well as in Vancouver's hottest cocktail bar and lab, Botanist. Born and raised in Melbourne, Australia, Sceney began bartending at the age of 18. After working in the industry for over eight years, he discovered his passion for bartending working at an exclusive five-star property. Sceney made his way to British Columbia in 2009 and worked in Whistler during the 2010 Winter Games before relocating to Vancouver which he now calls home.

Since arriving at Fairmont Pacific Rim, Grant has been integral in designing the internationally-regarded cocktail program of The Lobby Lounge. Now overseeing the hotel program, Grant uses a classic style with an avant-garde approach to cocktail development and design. He oversaw cocktail development in spring 2017 for its newest restaurant, Botanist. When asked to design his dream bar, he selected a variety of culinary-forward equipment for the country's most creative and innovative cocktail lab. His team's artistic studio is designed to inspire creativity, allowing the attention to detail required to forge an elevated drinking experience.

Since its inception, the Botanist Bar has been recognized internationally on the *Condé Nast Traveler* Hot List as one of the World's Best New Bars and at the Tales of the Cocktail Spirited Awards as one of the Best New Bars (Americas). Grant has been named Bartender of the Year at *Vancouver Magazine*'s 2016 Restaurant Awards and was awarded 2014 Diageo World Class Canada Bartender of the Year. He then went on that year to represent Canada in the World Class finals in the United Kingdom, where he finished with an impressive fourth place. Grant is an active member in the BC chapter of the CPBA as the education director, and actively participates on the cocktail competition circuit.

CANDY CAP MAGIC***

2 oz (60 ml) Candy cap-infused rye (p. 190)
¾ oz (22.5 ml) sweet vermouth (Noilly Prat Rouge)
¼ oz (7.5 ml) Root beer syrup (p. 204)
1 dash of Bittered Sling Kensington Bitters

Glass: Old-Fashioned / Rocks
Method: Stir all ingredients with ice and strain
Advanced serve option: Serve inside a terrarium on a bed of dry ice
and moss. Lace dry ice with essential oils of petrichor / rain essence.
Add warm water to create steam, close terrarium to create fog above
moss then serve
Garnish: None

REECE SIMS

Noted as the Best Bartender 2018 in Vancouver by *Populist Media*, Reece has a flair for over-garnished cocktails and creating unique imbibing experiences. He has worked as a bartender in all types of venues, including pubs, nightclubs, fine-dining restaurants, and cocktail bars such as most recently The Diamond.

Reece was selected as one of 10 Thirst Boston Scholars in 2017 and possesses a number of certifications including the Executive Bourbon Stewardship, Irish Whiskey Academy Discoverer Course, and WSET Level 3. In addition to bartending, Reece is the founder of Whiskey Muse, a website and YouTube channel that redefines the way whisk(e)y education is imparted. From educational pieces and infographics to cocktail recipes and videos, Whiskey Muse provides whisk(e)y education for enthusiasts in an unconventional, fun, easy-to-understand way.

THE FORT YORK*

1 ½ oz (45 ml) American rye whiskey (Woodford Reserve)
½ oz (15 ml) Fernet-Branca
1 oz (30 ml) lime juice
2/3 oz (20 ml) orgeat syrup (BG Reynolds)
6 fresh mint leaves

Glass: Large Cocktail
Method: Shake all ingredients with ice and double strain
Garnish: Mint sprig

KAITLYN STEWART

Kaitlyn Stewart began bartending 12 years ago when she found her passion for making great experiences and excellent drinks for her customers. Born in Toronto, she got into bartending as a means to help pay for university but fell in love with the craft and is now based at the Royal Dinette in Vancouver. A fan of shaking up a wide selection of innovative yet approachable drinks, Kaitlyn loves to incorporate local spirits and seasonal ingredients, creating delicious cocktails along the way.

Kaitlyn entered Diageo World Class in 2017, competing and winning the Canadian round and then joining 56 bartenders for the global finals in Mexico City. After an intense week of competition Kaitlyn won the global title of World Class Bartender of the Year, making her the first Canadian and second woman ever to win the prestigious title.

SPILT MILK***

1 ½ oz (45 ml) bourbon (Bulleit)
¼ oz (7.5 ml) amaretto (Sons of Vancouver)
¾ oz (22.5 ml) Milk liqueur
(p. 200)
½ oz (15 ml) lemon juice
¾ oz (22.5 ml) Cherry shrub
(p. 192)
2 dashes Angostura bitters
1/2 pinch of coarse salt

Glass: Milk Jug or Collins
Method: Shake all ingredients with ice and double strain over crushed ice
Garnish: Lemon twist and ginger cookie

JUSTIN TAYLOR

Justin is now in his twenty-fifth year in the service industry. He started making pizzas in small town Ontario before finding his passion in bartending, moving his family to Vancouver in 2007, and landing a high-profile job at the Four Seasons Hotel. There, he learned the art of drink making from hard work and perseverance, creating a world-class bar in a world-class hotel. He eventually found his own style and began making drinks that had purpose and a story.

Justin has a rule of always being the best in any role, while also conceding to the fact he may never be the best: the pursuit becomes the motivation. He has since stepped out from behind the bar and taken a general manager job at a great local cocktail bar, Cascade Room. He now mentors a new generation of bartenders, focusing on service first and empowering each one to develop their own style. For Justin, drink making is an art form, and developing personal style and techniques are an integral part of showcasing a personal journey and story. It doesn't really matter how one gets to the final destination; it only matters that one makes it and the journey is something that can be regarded with pride.

VANDUSEN SOUR*

2 oz (60 ml) akvavit (Sheringham)
½ oz (15 ml) elderflower liqueur (St. Germain)
½ oz (15 ml) vanilla liqueur (Giffard Vanilla de Madagascar)
1 oz (30 ml) lemon juice
3 dashes Peychaud's bitters
1 egg white

Glass: Large Cocktail
Method: Hard shake all ingredients with ice and double strain
Garnish: Express lemon zest and discard; add dehydrated edible flowers

DAVID WOLOWIDNYK

With a little over three decades of professional service experience both in front and behind the bar, David has recently embarked on a slightly new path, one that utilizes his extensive experience, education, accomplishments, and accolades—he is now a distiller of fine spirits. Currently, David is one of the distillers, the general manager, and the bar manager at Resurrection Spirits in Vancouver. David is also the cocktail stylist for *Taste Magazine*, and often writes articles about spirits for the *Publican Magazine*.

David is widely considered to be one of the pioneers of craft cocktail culture in Canada, both winning and judging regional, national, and international cocktail competitions. He was also a founding member, director, and treasurer of the CPBA. No stranger to the media, he's previously been named Bartender of the Year by both *Vancouver Magazine* and Urban Diner Restaurant Awards, as well as one of the Top 40 Foodies under 40 by *Western Living Magazine*. He also makes regular appearances on *Global BC News* demonstrating cocktails.

With distinction in his studies through both the ISG and the WSET, David is also a CSS Instructor for the Society of Wine Educators (SWE) and formerly a judge at the Vancouver International Spirit Competition.

GIN JULIUS*

1 ½ oz (45 ml) gin (Resurrection Spirits)
1 oz (30 ml) orange juice
¾ oz (22.5 ml) lemon juice
½ oz (15 ml) orgeat
¾ oz (22.5 ml) egg white

Glass: Large Cocktail
Method: Shake all ingredients vigorously with ice and single strain
Garnish: Light sprinkle of cinnamon in the center of the cocktail

CALEDONIA WRIGHT

Since childhood, Caledonia Wright has grown up with an innate sensibility toward taste and texture. Luckily, her hypersensitive persona has flourished in the food and beverage industry. Pairing this with her background in hospitality, Wright has developed a unique reputation for being highly intuitive when designing bespoke cocktails for her guests.

Starting her career in the pubs of downtown Toronto, Wright moved in 2007 to the west coast. Since then, she has worked behind several prominent bars in Victoria, with her last permanent position at Veneto Tapa Lounge in the prestigious Rialto Hotel. In 2017, Wright won first place in Speed Rack Canada's regionals and the Grand Marnier Cup in Whistler. Leaving her full-time position in May 2018, Wright is now working as a freelance bartender while she completes her degree in Professional Communication at Royal Roads University.

SEA WITCH*

1 ½ oz (45 ml) blanco tequila (Don Julio)
½ oz (15 ml) Aperol
½ oz (15 ml) medium-dry sherry (Alvear)
1/8 oz (3.75 ml) crème de pêche (Giffard)
Pinch of smoked sea salt

Glass: Small Cocktail / Nick & Nora
Method: Stir all ingredients with ice and strain
Garnish: Mezcal mist and dried nori

CAROLYN YU

The daughter of two people who don't drink, Carolyn had little early exposure to restaurant or bar culture. Having developed artistic talent at a young age, she chose the path to become a tattoo artist, but missed the energy of a buzzing room and meeting new people, so she found herself first on the dining room floor and eventually behind the bar. A trip to the Bar Convent Berlin show in 2015 opened her perspective on the different styles of bartending. It was there that she developed a deep interest in the eaux-de-vie of France, Germany and Switzerland and the amaro of Italy.

She's been very fortunate to have been mentored by some of the best in the business. Her very first coach impressed upon her that the pinnacle of being a good bartender is being well rounded, and that a bartender is an asset to the guests' experience. If you're incredible at making drinks but can't keep your guests happy or your station clean, you're doing it wrong.

Beyond the bar, Carolyn still runs a tattoo business at a private studio, donating proceeds to charities such as Mission Blue-Sylvia Earle Alliance, a global coalition with a goal to protect a worldwide network of marine protected areas, and Mind the Bar, a mental health resource and support system designed for those in hospitality that focuses on depression, addiction, and harassment.

THE WHITE WITCH***

1 ½ oz (45 ml) gin (Martin Miller)
½ oz (15 ml) Spruce tip tincture
(p. 207)
2/3 oz (20 ml) Spiced Riesling syrup
(p.20)
7
Glass: Green Chartreuse-rinsed
Small Cocktail / Nick & Nora
Method: Stir ingredients with ice
and strain
Garnish: Small square of Turkish
delight on the side

OFF THE BEATEN PATH:

OKANAGAN

A FOUR- TO SIX-HOUR drive east from Vancouver takes you directly into British Columbia's wine country. The Okanagan is a well-known wine region stretching for hundreds of kilometres from north to south, townships dotted along tourist drives spread along long stretches of highway wrapping its way around the lake. The larger urban areas are the epitome of the "Off the Beaten Path" element of this book and have seen an obvious resurgence of cocktail culture, with passionate bartenders pushing the envelope in their respective venues. The wine and culinary scene has encouraged the populace to expect quality drinks, and the bartenders of the Okanagan have responded unanimously.

JONATHON COTE

Raised in the restaurant industry since age 15, Jon got inspired to become a chef by a close relative. He attended culinary school and made his way to big hotels in the Bow Valley such as Fairmont Banff Springs and Chateau Lake Louise. Passionate about the industry, he decided to cross train as a server, where he discovered a passion for wines. This led him to the Okanagan where he met likeminded individuals who inspired him to bring back his culinary skills and apply them to cocktails. One of his biggest inspirations was a trip to Vancouver's Shameful Tiki, which reminded him a little bit of his childhood in Montréal.

During the '80s his parents used to bring him to Chinese restaurants where he was served tiki mocktails which came with many garnishes, flames, and umbrellas, which was always a treat at the time. Combining his love of crafting libations, creating locally sourced dishes as well as a fond respect of his community, Jon opened his own place in Penticton named Craft Corner Kitchen. Now three years in business, Jon is involved in promoting the local cocktail scene, working closely with fellow trade professionals, and providing urban offerings in a rural community.

SWEET SCIOLOM NARAMATA**

1 oz (30 ml) BC gin (Legend Distilling Doctors Orders)
1oz (30 ml) brandy (Maple Leaf Spirits Lady of the Cask)
1oz (30 ml) Lime cordial (p. 200)
Top with ginger beer

Glass: Highball / Collins
Method: Shake all ingredients with ice except ginger beer and strain over fresh ice. Top with ginger beer
Garnish: None

HARRY DOSANJ

Born and raised in Southampton, England, Harry's family decided to move to Canada in 2008 in search of a new life. With no experience in the food and beverage industry, his family opened a small restaurant in Kelowna called Poppadoms Taste India! Harry took over the bartender role, where he quickly realized that there's more to this than pouring pints and serving wine; he discovered cocktails. As he learnt more about cocktails and spirits, he started using his artistic skills and passion to create beautiful-looking beverages that taste great too.

Harry is a locally-celebrated bartender, a blogger for Tourism Kelowna, and his company Bar Travelling Man provides bartending services around town, from cocktail classes and event hire to bar and menu consulting.

LA JOYAU CACHE (HIDDEN GEM)**

1oz (30 ml) bourbon (Maker's Mark)
1oz (30 ml) Averna Amaro
1oz (30 ml) lemon juice
¾ oz (22.5 ml) Peach honey ginger syrup (p. 202)
6 fresh mint leaves

Glass: Large Cocktail
Method: Shake all ingredients with ice and double strain
Garnish: Sprig of mint

MARK MATSON

Born in Mirimichi, New Brunswick and raised in Sarnia, Ontario, Mark developed his legendary east coast hospitality roots from a young age, working everything from weddings to bingo halls. He caught the ski bum bug from there and found himself in Western Canada, working in fine dining establishments in everything from ski resorts to lakeside hotels, and even on a local Okanagan cruise boat. Wanting to further his passion, Mark made his way to Australia where he spent years learning from industry leaders.

Upon his return to the valley, Mark caught wind of a burgeoning mixology movement in the Okanagan and set his sights on what truly excited him: cocktails. When he's not competing in national cocktail competitions, he's the bar manager of two properties under the Nixon Hospitality Group as well as cocktail ambassador for Southern Comfort.

SUFFERIN' HEAT*

2 oz (60 ml) Southern Comfort
1 oz (30 ml) plum wine
¾ oz (22.5 ml) lime juice
½ oz Honey syrup (p. 197)
3 dashes apple cider vinegar
3 dashes absinthe (Okanagan Spirits Taboo Absinthe)
3 slices fresh ginger

Glass: Highball / Collins
Method: Muddle ginger in shaker, add ingredients, shake with ice and strain over fresh ice
Garnish: Mint sprig

IN FOCUS

DAVE SIMPSON & GERRY JOBE
SIMPS MIXERS

Born in Kelowna and raised between the Okanagan and the Shuswap, Gerry Jobe returned from years in Vancouver earning his stripes as a bartender and went on a mission to create a cocktail culture in the Okanagan. Endlessly creative, Gerry has won several awards for his cocktailing over the years and is responsible for spearheading the cocktail movement in British Columbia's wine country. He shifted his focus from competition to working with his peers in the community to encourage a field-to-glass approach to cocktails, utilizing every aspect of the Okanagan's bounty.

His passion for cocktails now has shifted again into a warlock's approach, utilizing frozen bones as ice cubes, aromatic feathers as garnishes, stirring creations in vibrating Tibetan Singing Bowls, and even smoking his syrups in a 200-year-old native *kekuli* in the center of a drum circle under the full moon during the winter solstice. High-concept cocktails inspired by pop-culture, film, literature, art, music, and Okanagan folklore have always been Gerry's niche, and every cocktail he creates has a story as its most essential ingredient.

Dave Simpson has been at the forefront of performance bartending for many years. Starting off working at the infamous Roxy Cabaret on Granville St., Dave too returned to the Okanagan to mentor and elevate the local bar scene. Dave's own bar, Avenue in Kelowna, was a legendary local spot for years, and during that time he showcased his skills on *The Rachael Ray Show*, at the Masters Golf Tournament at Augusta, and the Playboy Mansion. Dave also created Flairfest, Canada's longest-running bartender competition, bringing the best in North America together in the Okanagan and Vancouver for a whopping 13 years.

Together, Jobe and Simpson linked up to energize the local bar scene and to create Simps Syrups. The inspiration for Simp's is due to the influx of cocktail culture across bars and restaurants without a proper cocktail program.

Their custom syrups are designed to provide establishments with bartender-designed syrups for consistency and ease of use, as well as to alleviate the associated labour costs involved in daily production of ingredients. Simp's also created Simp's Serious Caesar Mix the first vegan, gluten-free, no-MSG Caesar mix and have recently launched Dill Pickle and Sriracha versions. Jobe and Simpson partnered with Richard Nixon, an expert on scaling business, and with their new CEO in place they have signed on with the Pattison Group for listing in their stores across Canada. They recently opened their new production facility and retail shop in Kelowna.

BONE BRIGADE BY GERRY JOBE**

2 oz (60 ml) bourbon
(Woodford Reserve)
½ oz (15 ml) Simp's
Blackberry Vanilla Cream
Syrup
5 dashes Bittered Sling Plum
& Rootbeer Bitters

Glass: Old-Fashioned / Rocks
Method: Stir with ice and
strain over frozen femur bone
Garnish: None

GIN GIN SOUTHSIDE BY DAVE SIMPSON**

2 oz (60 ml) gin
1 oz (30 ml) Simp's Ginger, Cucumber & Lime Syrup
Top with soda

Glass: Old-Fashioned / Rocks
Method: Shake all ingredients expect
soda with ice and strain over fresh ice
Garnish: Mint foam (p. 200), slice of
cucumber, and a rose petal

ALBERTA

CALGARY and Edmonton are only 280 kilometers apart, with as many similarities as there are differences. Both cities are culminations of extremes: Bitter cold winters, blistering hot summers, money-rich oil fields, and urban centres fueled by extravagance. As a hub for many primary industries in the country, it has become a bastion in the Rockies for good food and wine with cocktails not too far behind. Many of Vancouver's amazing bartenders were born and bred in Alberta and made the move, while many young bartenders saw the option of staying and creating an oasis in the areas that surround the downtown cores.

Local distilleries have exploded in the province, fueling bartenders to showcase their products and partner with them to create unique and distinct spirits for their bars. Both cities are evolving at a drastic pace—the volume of new bars and restaurants that are filled with enthusiastic, talented staff is astounding.

CALGARY

CALGARY has been, and will be for the foreseeable future, an oil town. As a primary industry city, the style of restaurant has always been geared towards the wealthy oil workers on their days off. But as the diversity of workers has spread into the peripheral needs of the energy industry, including government and tech, so has the clientele. Gone are the days of expensive steaks with California Cabernet—although still prevalent; a group of talented bartenders and chefs have begun to give Calgary a renaissance that they didn't think they needed. Slowly but surely over the last decade, cocktail bars have popped up and changed the way people drink. Was it called upon by creative bartenders or knowledgeable guests who made the move to the city for work? No one knows, but they are all happy that it has happened with such great success. Calgary is a big city with a tight-knit community, and the attention they have received is well deserved.

DYLAN AIKINS

Dylan Aikins began his career at the tender age of 20 years old at a local beer pub called Bottlescrew Bills, naively hoping that his love of Belgian tripels would eventually manifest itself into a job as a brewer. However, before stumbling too far down the craft beer road, he found himself on a bar stool at Model Milk, where the service and cocktails profoundly resonated with him. He was able to talk the management behind Model Milk to let him behind the bar, and shortly after was a founding team member of its sister bar Pigeonhole.

His residency hammered home a love for obscure classics, forming the core foundations of his drink making along with a new adoration of Riesling and fortified wine. Craving more creative freedom brought him to Ricardo's Hideaway, where he was swallowed whole by the world of rum and Hawaiian shirts. He recently came full circle back to his craft beer roots and can be found behind the wood at Last Best Brewery and Distillery. He has been funnelling everything he's learned over the past half a decade into proving that even a brewpub can have incredible cocktails, collaborating with brewers and distillers who are just as passionate about what they put into the glass as he is.

FREE RADICALS**

1 ½ oz (45 ml) Sarsaparilla-
infused Flor de Cana 4 year
(p. 206)
½ oz (15 ml) amontillado sherry
¾ oz (22.5 ml) Sage syrup
(p. 205)
1 oz (30 ml) lime juice
2 dashes Banana and clove
bitters

Glass: Absinthe-rinsed Large
Cocktail
Method: Shake all ingredients
with ice and double strain
Garnish: Grated nutmeg

DAVID BAIN

Once described as a "Service Swiss Army knife" with more than 25 years of hospitality, David has had the opportunity to work in every possible position in a restaurant just short of being a chef. In the last 12 years, he has dedicated himself to the bar. Investing in his continuing knowledge, he has completed WSET Levels 2 and 3, BarSmarts, and CSS. With multiple excursions throughout the world in the form of branded trips, Tales of the Cocktail, and Camp Runamok, he is eternally grateful for this job taking him around the world.

THE MAN FROM MEZCAL*

1 oz (30 ml) mezcal
(Koch Espadin)
1 oz (30ml) reposado
tequila
1 oz (30ml) Cynar
2 dashes Regans' Orange
Bitters No. 6

Glass: Large Cocktail
Method: Stir all
ingredients with ice and
strain
Garnish: Orange twist

MAYA BARTHA

Growing up on the west coast of Washington state, Maya Bartha learned an appreciation for fresh ingredients at a young age. Upon moving to Calgary in 2010, she began her career in the restaurant industry, starting in casual fine-dining Italian and French restaurants. She embarked upon her journey into the cocktail world when she joined the opening team at Proof Cocktail Bar. This ignited an enduring passion for cocktails and spirits. She defines her cocktail style as "whimsical and playful in presentation, but simple in execution". She believes that atmosphere and service play just as important a role in the conversation between the guest and bartender as the cocktail itself. Maya is currently running the bar program at Shelter cocktail bar in Calgary.

THE NORTHERN LIGHTS**

1 ½ oz (45 ml) Sage-infused Empress 1908 Gin (p. 205)
½ oz (15 ml) Burwood Medica Honey Liqueur
¼ oz (7.5 ml) Chamomile & lavender syrup (p. 191)
1 barspoon Citric acid solution (p. 193)

Glass: Large Cocktail
Method: Stir all ingredients with ice and strain
Garnish: Fresh sage leaf

DINAH KISIL

Dinah Kisil first became interested in bartending while she completed her honors degrees in social justice and psychology at Bishop's University in Sherbrooke, Quebec. While studying, she often travelled to bigger cities on the weekends to take in the independent nightlife cultures. After becoming a regular at the legendary Le Mal Nécessaire in Montréal, she became familiar with the local bartending scene and began learning more about bartending culture. After completing her degrees, she moved to Calgary and went into restaurant management.

After a year of self-teaching plus feverishly reading cocktail and bartending books, she left hospitality management and pursued bartending at Calgary's first exclusively rum-focused cocktail bar. From there she proceeded to develop her skills, running a few successful cocktail programs throughout Calgary before settling down at one of the top five of Canada's top 50 cocktail bars: Proof Cocktail Bar. Taking inspiration from her community, Dinah continuously strives to positively contribute to Calgary's cocktail culture by consistently bringing awareness to local sociocultural problems through initiatives and non-profit partnerships.

DEMURE THOUGHTS*

1 ½ oz (45 ml) Plantation Pineapple Rum
½ oz (15 ml) peated Scotch whisky
1/3 oz (10 ml) Campari
¾ oz (22.5 ml) lime juice
¼ oz (7.5 ml) Heavy syrup (p. 210)

Glass: Large Cocktail
Method: Shake all ingredients with ice and double strain
Garnish: None

MAKINA LABRECQUE

Makina's love of food, wine and spirits brought her to the Calgary hospitality industry after years of performing professionally as an Irish dancer. After working her way through many industry jobs in all positions, Makina finally found herself working her dream job at Proof Cocktail Bar. Two-and-a-half years later, she has progressed from bartender to bar manager/head bartender and is now currently in the general/bar manager and creative director position.

Makina has gone on to compete in and win many local and national cocktail competitions, most recently representing Canada in the 2017 and 2018 Patrón Perfectionists global final. When she isn't at the bar you can find her organizing hospitality-related community initiatives. Her favorite cocktail is the Margarita. She believes it transcends prevention: It's an airport cocktail, a party cocktail, and a cocktail that can test the skills of a great bartender.

WILD ROSE MARGARITA*

1 ½ oz (45 ml) blanco tequila (Patrón Silver)
½ oz (15 ml) Patrón Citronge Orange
1 oz (30 ml) rosé vermouth (Cocchi Rosa)
½ oz (15 ml) gin (Bombay Sapphire)
½ oz (15 ml) lime juice
½ oz (15 ml) Simple syrup (p. 209)
1 dash rose water

Glass: Large Cocktail
Method: Shake all ingredients with ice and double strain
Garnish: Fanned strawberry

MADELEINE MACDONALD

Madeleine has been in the hospitality industry for over 12 years, and fell in love with cocktails after starting a job as a bartender at Model Milk in Calgary. She went on to compete and win Mademoiselle Cointreau Alberta in 2014. Madeleine was soon after named Beverage Director at Model Milk, Pigeonhole, and Model Citizen as well as named one of the top 5 people to watch in Calgary's food scene in 2016. After leaving Model Milk, Madeleine helped open Calcutta Cricket Club and recently won a White Hat award for outstanding service in beverage as well as being nominated for the 2018 Mayor's White Hat award. She continues to inspire the next generation of hospitality professionals in her role as food and beverage service instructor at SAIT Polytechnic.

GOODBYE HORSES**

1 ½ oz (45 ml) bourbon (Buffalo Trace)
½ oz (15 ml) elderflower liqueur (St. Germain)
1oz (30 ml) lemon juice
¾ oz (22.5 ml) Gewürztraminer syrup (p. 196)
2 dashes Angostura bitters
1 dash Scrappy's Cardamom Bitters

Glass: Large Cocktail
Method: Shake all ingredients with ice and double strain
Garnish: None

ALLIE MARTIN

Allie got into cocktail bartending by chance: It's been a little over a year since she ran her first real service behind the wood and had the pleasure of getting a cocktail in print on a menu. She has always been a curious and creative creature, which is why she is comfortable tackling this ever-growing industry. She discovered her love for cocktail competitions, which fed her curiosity for pushing the boundaries when it comes to flavour combinations. Mezcal became her vice, as it taught her what her palate enjoys and what strange pairings she could create. She currently resides at Milk Tiger.

GOOD DAYS, BAD DAYS**

1 ½ oz (45 ml) mezcal (Koch Espadin)
¾ oz (22.5 ml) banana liqueur
¼ oz (7.5 ml) Heavy syrup (p. 210)
¾ oz (22.5 ml) lime juice
3 dashes Long pepper tincture (p. 200)
1 oz (30 ml) Phillips Blue Buck Beer

Glass: Old-Fashioned / Rocks
Method: Shake all ingredients with ice except beer and strain over rocks. Top up with beer.
Garnish: None

JIMMY NGUYEN

Jimmy started off bartending with the age-old tale about a university student trying to pay off his loans, only to still be bartending after graduating with a bachelor's degree in health and physical education. After spending eight years working behind the bar, Jimmy has placed highly in major cocktail competitions and now tries to fold his degree into bartending by looking at the health and wellness side of things for people in the industry.

Jimmy enjoys how cocktails and beverages can bridge the gap between himself and a guest so that the guest feels comfortable enough to talk about themselves and their issues. For Jimmy, bartending is more than just creating drinks and serving guests; there is a culture behind it too.

THE UPPER LEFT***

1 ½ oz (45 ml) gin (Bombay Sapphire)
¾ oz (22.5 ml) Amaro Montenegro
½ oz (15 ml) rosé vermouth (Cocchi Rosa)
¼ oz (7.5 ml) Brown butter-washed, cold-brew coffee and honey syrup (p. 190)

Glass: Old-Fashioned / Rocks
Method: Toss all ingredients with ice eight times
Garnish: Lemon twist expressed and discarded

TIMO SALIMAKI

Timo Salimaki is originally from St. Albert. His family made the move to Calgary when he was 18, and he has been working in and around the restaurant industry with his family for the last 15 years. His brother is a chef and Timo worked the front of house. He got his big break working with chef Michael Noble at Catch Restaurant when it won *enRoute* magazine's #1 Best New Restaurant in Canada.

Timo has a long career working and opening many restaurants, he has done every job that the front of house has to offer from server's assistant, bartender, server, and shift leader, to assistant manager, general manager, and director of operations. Wine was always a passion until he discovered the wonderful world of cocktails. He has competed in cocktail competitions with great success: He was fortunate enough to win 2017 Bombay Sapphire's Most Imaginative Bartender in Canada along with placing third in Bacardi Legacy and 2016 Grey Goose Pour Masters. Being creative is an outlet that he truly loves.

THE MIREPOIX EXPERIENCE***

2 oz (60 ml) gin (Bombay Sapphire)
1 ¾ oz (52.5 ml) Mirepoix soup (p. 200)
½ oz (15 ml) orange liqueur (Cointreau)
¼ oz (7.5 ml) lemon juice
½ oz (15 ml) Honey ginger syrup (p. 198)
2 dashes celery bitters

Glass: Large Cocktail
Method: Shake all ingredients with ice and double strain
Garnish: Parmesan tuile (p. 202)

FRANZ SWINTON

Franz has been bartending since 2001, but it was after a stint abroad in Dubai where he found his passion for cocktails and service. He returned to Calgary in 2006 with his newfound knowledge and the intention of growing the cocktail culture in his beloved city. It was at this point that he sought out his soon-to-be mentor Graham Warner and employment at Raw Bar in Hotel Arts—arguably the birthplace and focal point for the birth of Calgary's cocktail scene. The upcoming years saw Franz compete and find much success in local, national and international cocktail competitions.

Franz has been seen as one of the forefathers of Calgary's now exploding cocktail community. He was the first president of the Calgary Bartenders Association, which eventually became the Alberta chapter of the CPBA. You can currently catch Franz either organizing or judging the majority of the local cocktail competitions. His focus is still set on building the community and fostering growth amongst enthusiastic bartenders and industry professionals in Alberta.

PARADISO**

1 ½ oz (45 ml) gin (Bombay Sapphire)
½ oz (15 ml) Campari
1/3 oz (10 ml) Roasted fennel syrup (p. 204)
1oz (30 ml) lemon juice
3 drops Firenze tincture (p. 195)

Glass: Large Cocktail
Method: Shake all ingredients with ice and double strain
Garnish: Fennel fronds

GREG WILLIAMS

Originally hailing from Down Under and looking for a change from academia, Greg was thrown in the deep end for his first serious bartending gig at a quirky little Japanese place that didn't last too long: Two weeks of being shown the ropes and then left to run the bar solo every day and night for the next year. This experience, along with his own research and experimentation, eventually led to a spot on the team at Bridgette Bar where he worked his way up to oversee the venue and its cocktail program.

Greg likes to explore unexpected or interesting combinations that surprise the palate or challenge expectations. He says Tiger Moth reminds him of the flavours and aromas of his native land—Australia.

TIGER MOTH*

1 ½ oz (45 ml) bourbon
(Buffalo Trace)
¾ oz (22.5 ml) Aperol
1 oz (30 ml) pineapple juice
½ oz (15 ml) Citric acid
solution (p. 193)

Glass: Large Cocktail
Method: Shake all
ingredients with ice and
double strain
Garnish: Rose water spritz

EDMONTON

EDMONDTON is a city that has always been a little too far north, and a little too out of the way. As a result, the artistic, musical, and culinary communities of Edmonton have always needed to sustain themselves. This has led to the city's immense creativity and DIY approach to things. The cocktail culture here is no different. Most of the original founders here moved on to other cities after training a few bartenders, or decided to step back from active mentorship.

However, these bartenders blazed a trail, showing what was possible. Now, young bartenders have taken up the mantle of that DIY approach to expanding their craft. Unsurprisingly, it's yielded remarkable results. Edmonton has started to gain national attention for its passionate, hospitable, and engaging bar culture. While we still may have to travel to Calgary or Vancouver to compete against our peers, more often than not we come home the victor. Though still a young market, Edmonton is driven, hungry, and ready to show the rest of the country what we can do.— James Grant

ANDRÉ VAN BOBER

André started out in the cocktail world by applying for a job at Woodwork, where he was taken on at the same time as fellow bartender Natasha Trowsdale. In his time at Woodwork he had the opportunity to learn from Jeff Savage, Natasha, Clayton Kozak, and James Grant. After Woodwork, he took on the bar manager position at Baijiu, a venue that has been huge for the Edmonton cocktail scene in terms of creating a space that has a very laid-back vibe with the same quality cocktails and variety you would experience at any other high-end cocktail bar/restaurant.

A year after opening Baijiu André opened up Edmonton's first speakeasy, Little Hong Kong. The bar team was a mix of Edmonton's Who's Who. He feels that he is the luckiest person alive to have worked with so many amazing bartenders over so many years in such a small yet amazing cocktail city.

KOWLOON BLOOD ALLEY*

1 oz (30 ml) cognac
(Hennessy VS)
½ oz (15 ml) Campari
½ oz (15 ml) mezcal
½ oz (15 ml) ruby port
½ oz (15 ml) The King's Ginger

Glass: Old-Fashioned / Rocks
Method: Stir all ingredients with ice and strain over a large cube
Garnish: Lemon twist

JORDAN CLEMENS

Jordan's start as a bartender was very fortuitous, he worked in a café during university that happened to have one of the best European/Craft beer selections in Edmonton at the time. The owner also had a taste for amaro and grappa. He found himself constantly tasting new and interesting things. His love for coffee naturally was displaced onto cocktails as he fell down the rabbit hole—he fell in love with the history, the traditions, the knowledge, and the creativity of the craft. Coming from an academic and a musical background, he naturally adapted to the challenges of cocktail bartending.

After a brief foray into graduate school and academic research, he found himself back in Edmonton in early 2013 bartending at the nascent Three Boars, which in many ways helped create the cocktail culture in Edmonton. This is where he was constantly experimenting and travelling to learn more about spirits and cocktails. After Three Boars, he helped open Woodwork at which he is now a partner, all while gaining his CSS and WSET Level 3 certifications and developing a keen interest in wine. Two-and-a-half years ago, he opened Clementine, which was recognized as the fifth best new restaurant in Canada in 2018 by *enRoute* magazine. Both restaurants have excellent cocktail, wine, and spirit programs, for which he is very proud and still helps oversee while still working behind the bar several nights a week.

TIERRA*

1 oz (30 ml) mezcal (Peloton de la Muerte)
1 oz (30 ml) Ancho Reyes
1oz (30 ml) Don's Mix (p. 194)
½ oz (15 ml) fresh lime
2 dashes Scrappy's Celery Bitters
3 oz (90 ml) Pilsner Urquell

Glass: Highball / Collins
Method: Shake all ingredients except Pilsner Urquell with ice, add beer and strain over fresh ice
Garnish: Grapefruit half slice and a half rim of ancho powder

104

JAMES GRANT

A relatively young and extremely talented addition to Edmonton's bartending community, James Grant has been 'tending for the last six years. After getting his start in London, James moved home and was lucky enough to start at Woodwork—the premiere cocktail bar in the city at the time. Working from barback up to bar manager, James was able to build his skills and grow significantly. He's since moved on to work at the best bars the city has to offer.

James has pushed himself to compete whenever possible with the understanding that competitions push bartenders outside of their comfort zones and force them to grow. Every time he's competed, he's returned better able to serve his guests, because the guest is what it is all about.

OLD GREY RABBIT*

1 ¾ oz (52.5 ml) single pot still Irish whiskey (Power's Signature or Redbreast 12 year)
¼ oz (7.5 ml) apricot brandy (Giffard)
¼ oz (7.5 ml) Bénédictine DOM
¼ oz (7.5 ml) oloroso sherry
½ oz (15 ml) amber vermouth (Noilly Prat)
2 dashes Dale DeGroff Pimento bitters

Glass: Small Cocktail
Method: Stir all ingredients with ice and strain
Garnish: Orange twist

TYLER GUSHATY

Born and raised in Edmonton, Tyler first got his foot in the hospitality industry at age 14 and after growing tired of washing dishes, he found himself with a busboy job at The Keg Steakhouse and Bar. This is where he realized the intrigue of bartending, helping as a bar assist for a couple of years, which taught him many valuable lessons that carried him where he is today. Finally getting the chance to bartend legally he stepped up to the role of bartender as soon as he turned 18. Like most, it started as a casual evening gig to financially support him through university.

That evolved into jobs in any type of bartending venue imaginable: big corporate franchise restaurants, pubs, and nightclubs. It wasn't until early 2014 that he got his first job as a craft bartender under the infamous late Brendan Brewster at a small new restaurant called North53. That was the same point he decided to fully invest himself in a career as a bartender. Ending his tenure close to five years later as the general manager, he honed his skills in drink development, back office systems, and everything in between. In his opinion the sky is the limit in this trade, and he won't be looking back anytime soon.

ZEN GARDEN**

1 ½ oz (45 ml) blanco tequila (Espolon)
½ oz (15 ml) Aperol
¾ oz (22.5 ml) lemon juice
½ oz (15 ml) Strawberry syrup (p. 208)
¼ oz (7.5 ml) wasabi paste

Glass: Old-Fashioned / Rocks
Method: Shake all ingredients with ice and strain over fresh ice
Garnish: Mint sprig and a dehydrated strawberry slice

CHRIS KROCK

Chris started his career in the kitchen, quickly rising through the ranks and becoming a head chef for a few years. He then wanted to do front of house duties, mainly because one day he wanted to operate his own restaurant, and by knowing all sides he thought it would be beneficial to get into a front-of-house position. Back when he was front of house the notion of higher-end dining was pretty much nonexistent in Edmonton. Thus, like many others, he worked at a chain and became a bar manager. This is where his love and passion for cocktails and the culture around it started.

Since then he has gone on to general manage some of Edmonton's best restaurants and has continued to elevate his cocktail knowledge and involvement in the industry. He has gone on to win some great cocktails comps, write cocktail columns, as well as teach and develop new and existing restaurants as a territory manager for Southern Glazers Wine and Spirits. In the coming months he is moving into the role of western Canada mixology ambassador for luxury brands with Southern Glazers.

JIVE TURKEY**

1 ½ oz (45 ml) bourbon (Wild Turkey 101)
¼ oz (7.5 ml) sweet vermouth (Punt e Mes)
½ oz (15 ml) lime juice
1 barspoon Sour cherry jam (p. 207)
3 dashes smoked cherry bitters
1oz (30 ml) egg white

Glass: Smoked-cherry sugar half rimmed Small Cocktail / Nick & Nora
Method: Shake all ingredients with ice, dry shake and double strain
Garnish: Wild Turkey-soaked sour cherry

NATASHA TROWSDALE

Natasha began in the service industry in 2014 in Sherwood Park, Alberta. Originally hired as a server, she arrived to her first shift and was placed behind the bar due to staff shortage. She immediately felt at home behind the wood and after reading her first cocktail book *Death and Co.: Modern Classic Cocktails*, re-watching *Hey Bartender* every other night, and buying her first set of shaker tins, she found her calling and wanted to grow as a bartender.

She took the next step and applied for a long-shot job as server and barback at Woodwork and landed it. Along with the help of some amazing mentors she quickly became a full-time bartender on the team. Currently she is the general manager of one of Edmonton's most regarded cocktail bars, Baijiu, with other projects on the horizon.

TASH PASH*

1 ¼ oz (37.5 ml) blanco tequila (Casamigos)
¼ oz (7.5 ml) reposado tequila (Uno Mas)
½ oz (15 ml) passion fruit liqueur (Giffard)
¼ oz (7.5 ml) Licor 43
½ oz (15 ml) grapefruit juice
½ oz (15 ml) lime juice

Glass: Salt-rimmed Old-Fashioned / Rocks
Method: Shake all ingredients with ice and strain over fresh ice
Garnish: Grapefruit twist

EVAN WATSON

Evan Watson is a co-owner of Clementine, cocktail and wine columnist for CBC Radio Edmonton, and has been working in the hospitality industry ever since he was legally old enough to do so. Classic cocktails turned into a specific area of interest, after Evan become dejected at the mundanity of working in the corporate restaurant scene.

During an undergraduate degree in sociology and after being exposed to the writing of Walter Benjamin, he began lamenting the death of a pre-mass production artistic era from which he felt he'd been cheated. The laborious, individually-crafted cocktail was a suitable target on which to hitch his frustrations, and he slowly built out a home bar to help him procrastinate from writing papers. His first cocktail job was as an opening bartender at Woodwork under the mentorship of Brendan Brewster, which allowed him to meet his future business partners, Jordan Clemens and Andrew Barely, who together went on to open Clementine.

While the idea for Clementine was being formed, the trio operated a craft-cocktail pop-up service called The Volstead Act and Evan found a home behind Three Boars, Edmonton's original cult-cocktail bar.

With the opening of Clementine, Evan's trajectory grew, and he became immersed in the world of wine. In 2018, he won the Chaîne des Rôtisseurs Best Young Sommelier award for his region and now spends much of his time championing sustainable, human-scale farming in the wine industry by consulting with other restaurants, traveling to meet wine producers, and through his work with the CBC. Weather dependent, it is equally as likely you will find him with a cold Sazerac in his hands as you will with a bottle of cold Beaujolais.

FIRESHRINE**

½ oz (15 ml) mezcal (Del Maguey Vida)
2 oz (60 ml) Tepache (p. 208)
1 barspoon agave nectar
6 oz (180 ml) pilsner beer

Glass: Highball / Collins
Method: Build over ice
Garnish: Lime wedge

RED DEER

RED DEER is smack between Calgary and Edmonton, two of Canada's largest cities. It's Alberta's third largest city, and home to many bars and restaurants. It wasn't until To the Lost—Red Deer's first and only cocktail lounge that opened in the Spring of 2015—that cocktails started to play a part in the city's imbibing ways. In a city that has long prospered on cheap highballs and beer, To the Lost has given Red Deer employees and patrons alike a more refined palate and appreciation of a lost craft.

While it's still a growing scene, there aren't many respectable lounges you can go in this city that don't have a barkeep that wants to show you their newest creation. It's amazing to see a city population, that's been set in its ways for decades, saddle up to the wood, and start talking cocktails with the bartender. With local cocktail mentors like the ones showcased here helping groom up-and-coming bartenders that are hungry for cocktail knowledge, the local scene is in good hands.— Sean Draper

MATT BUCK

Matt started behind the bar in 2005 and after years of volume bartending and managing in pubs and restaurants, he opened To The Lost in 2015—Red Deer's first cocktail bar. To The Lost provided him the opportunity to really deepen his knowledge of spirits and cocktails and get in on the ground floor of Central Alberta's burgeoning cocktail scene.

In addition to his full-time position at To The Lost, he is also the owner of The Copper Stag Cocktail Company, where he caters private cocktail parties, teaches spirits and cocktail classes, and consults with bars and restaurants, most notably the award-winning Cilantro and Chive in Lacombe. He couldn't be prouder to be a small piece of central Alberta's culture of food and drink. The community is starting to develop a real passion for cocktails and they've only just begun. Matt can't wait to see what the future has in store.

COLLARED DOVE**

2 oz (60 ml) Pimm's
½ oz (15 ml) gin (Tanqueray No. Ten)
¼ oz (7.5 ml) Amaro dell'Erborista
¼ oz (7.5 ml) passion fruit liqueur (Giffard)
1 oz (30 ml) fresh lime juice
1 oz (30 ml) pineapple juice
1 oz (30 ml) Guava syrup (p. 197)
2 dashes blended orange bitters (Regans' No.6 and Fee Brothers Gin Barrel-Aged Orange)

Glass: Highball / Collins
Method: Shake all ingredients with ice and strain over crushed ice
Garnish: Cucumber wheel and 3 dried juniper berries

SEAN DRAPER

Sean has been involved in the industry for nearly 19 years, starting as a dishwasher at Airdie. Absentee staff created opportunities for him on the floor and eventually the bar, where he fell in love and found his calling. He moved to Red Deer a few years later for college and after growing fond of the city, stayed afterwards. He supported himself working in bars and clubs for several years, but it wasn't until a visit to his family in his hometown of Halifax in the fall of 2011 that he was introduced to the world of cocktails by Jenner Cormier. After this realization, he returned to Red Deer, knowing they needed better quality drinks and in 2015 opened To The Lost with Matt Buck.

WALKING THROUGH THE MEADOWS*

1 ½ oz (45 ml) bourbon (Woodford Reserve)
½ oz (15 ml) elderflower liqueur (St-Germain)
¾ oz (22.5 ml) fresh lime juice
½ oz (15 ml) Simple syrup (p. 209)
2 dashes Angostura bitters
4 fresh mint leaves
3 fresh raspberries

Glass: Large Cocktail
Method: Gently muddle 3 mint leaves and raspberries, add other ingredients, shake with ice and double strain
Garnish: Mint leaf

SETH VAN HAVERE

Seth Van Havere has been bartending in Red Deer since 2001—with a couple years in Vancouver in the early days—in nearly everywhere from family restaurant to dive bar to wine bar. A love of history and drink led him to read David Wondrich's *Imbibe* in 2011, creating a love of cocktails. Teaching classes and consulting with bars for staff training, he's trying to show a small market like Red Deer how amazing the world of cocktails can be. Seth currently tends bar at Bo's Bar & Stage.

LONESOME DOVE*

1 ½ oz (45 ml) cognac
(Courvoisier VS)
½ oz (15 ml) Yukon Jack
1 barspoon Chambord Royale
2 dashes orange bitters
Pinch of salt

Glass: Small Cocktail / Nick
& Nora
Method: Stir all ingredients
with ice and strain
Garnish: Lemon twist

SASKATCHEWAN

ONE OF THE COUNTRY'S central-most provinces situated between Alberta and Manitoba, Saskatchewan bills itself as the "Land of Living Skies" due to its relative geographical flatness, allowing for you to see for miles and miles unobstructed. Saskatoon is the city on the plain, small and unique. It is becoming a hot spot for tech companies, but with the backbone of producing most of Canada's grain supply. With the new and old intersecting, the use of local grains has created a fledgling craft spirits movement which has further fuelled the bartender's passion for local ingredients. Saskatchewan is truly the epitome of "if you build it, they will come".

SASKATOON

IF YOU ARE TRAVELLING across Canada, either for work or pleasure, it's time to stop skipping over Saskatoon and start making it an extended pit stop or destination. We will understand if you only call during the winter season, but we fully expect you to visit come summer. We aren't that awkward uncle you avoid who brings out his shotgun after a couple beers anymore; we are the other uncle, the one who's got tasty beef jerky from last year's hunt and hooch that actually tastes good! We've become fun.

Saskatoon's food-and-beverage scene has grown up and is now in its teenage years. Kyle Mathew and Christie Peters, owners of the Hollows and Primal, were arguably the two who began Saskatoon's changing of guard when it came to how and what Saskatoon ate. Back in 2011, Saskatoon was mostly filled with chain restaurants, pubs, and dancehall-style night clubs. A lot has changed since then: Gone are all but three of the night clubs, and local establishments dominate over the chains. We still have some old-school legit spots, but the tide has certainly shifted in the past 10 years.—Chad Coombs

CHAD COOMBS

Chad Coombs unknowingly began his bartending career in his late teens, long before ever setting foot behind a bar, for hosting get-togethers and parties at his home ignited the flame of hospitality within Coombs. After stepping foot behind his first bar in his late twenties to help finance his fine-art career, Coombs was immediately captivated. Every day was a party, every night a celebration, everyone was your friend.

Over the years, the parties and celebrations Coombs hosted from behind the bar evolved and grew with Saskatoon's emerging cocktail scene. Coombs' creativity started to flow from his fine-art career into his creative cocktails. Coombs has always considered himself a back-bar-style 'tender, from the flavored-vodka focused back bars when he started to the amaro focused ones he curates now. Not one to ever limit himself, however, Coombs is known for creating interesting ingredients such as a catnip syrup for his Catnip Daiquiri.

Coombs has been a leader in the Saskatoon community via his passion for sharing knowledge as well as bringing in others from outside Saskatoon to help inspire and grow the city's bartending community. Coombs has also been an important figure in growing Saskatoon's cocktail credentials far beyond its city limits. Whether through his bartending-focused travels, volunteer work, or his internationally-followed cocktail diary (@coqtale), Coombs hopes to continue sharing his prairie hospitality and to host from behind the bar for as long as he can.

THE SMOKING MONK*

1 oz (30 ml) Islay whisky (Laphroaig 10 year)
1 oz (30 ml) Green Chartreuse
1 raw sugar cube
4 dashes Peychaud's bitters
Absinthe rinse

Glass: Absinthe-rinsed Small Cocktail
Method: Muddle Peychaud's and raw sugar well, pour in Laphroaig and Green Chartreuse; stir with ice until chilled.
Garnish: Express lemon oils and garnish with lemon peel

KANDRA KERGEN

Kandra has been the bar manager, sommelier, and beverage director at The James Hotel in Saskatoon for the last five years along with studying for her WSET Diploma which she aims to complete in 2020. She began her career behind a bar in Amsterdam while backpacking through Europe: Desperate for some funds, she lied about her experience to get the job. After three months of bartending, she realized that a passion had been lit inside her. Bartending has since allowed her to travel and develop her professional identity throughout Australia, New Zealand, and England, which forced her to quickly adapt and learn about her environment.

After returning to Canada, she tried her hand at some late-night club bartending in Montréal and Saskatoon which was short-lived, as she grew to know that this was not her true bartending style. She finally found her home with craft cocktails and wine at The James Hotel in 2013 where she started managing the Lobby Bar in 2015 and hasn't looked back since. While she spends fewer days behind the wood, she gets to spend more time leading educational programs and collaborating with her team. This industry has been built on giving back and she is always looking to work with people who are new to the game or returning to it.

TERROIR***

2oz (60 ml) Crimini mushroom-infused cognac (Hennessy VS) (p. 193)
1/5 oz (5 ml) Thyme honey syrup (p. 208)
¼ oz (7.5 ml) Gala apple shrub (p. 195)
3 drops of portobello essence
1 dash of Bittered Sling Autumn Bog Bitters

Glass: Warmed Snifter
Method: Stir without ice and strain
Garnish: Crispy sage leaf

MANITOBA

MANITOBA is a vast province, almost the size of Texas, and covers the arctic tundra in the north all the way to the US border in the south. Like many provinces in the country, the diversity of cultures is immense. In Manitoba, Icelandic and Nordic culture is interestingly prevalent. This all began in the late 1800s and the eruption of Mount Askja in Iceland, which began the mass Nordic migration to Lake Manitoba. Thousands made the transition to Manitoba, especially to Gimli where there is a yearly Viking festival. Manitoba has gorgeous landscapes from frozen tundra to mountainous ranges and classic Canadian picture scapes.

WINNIPEG

THE FIRST TIME I went to Winnipeg was to do training at a local Keg Restaurant, I remember thinking just how much it resembled something like LA: A high-rise metropolis in the distance and spread out suburbs that stretched out over miles. I was staying in the outskirts of town close to the training venue and realized just how dispersed everything was when I looked up a coffee recommendation from a friend and it was a 20-minute drive—a 45-minute round trip for coffee was a lot, even for me.

The cocktail culture of Winnipeg is still relatively new and existed long before the guests that ventured to the cocktail-centric spaces were on the same level. But unperturbed, the pillars of the bar community built and struggled until cocktails became a new niche in the city's culinary scene. With the spread-out nature of the city, distilleries, restaurants, and cocktail bars have populated suburbs outside the city limits more than I have seen anywhere else in Canada. The neighborhood cocktail joint is alive and well in Winnipeg.

JOEL CARLETON

Joel Carleton has been in the hospitality industry for over 10 years, with five of those spent in competitive craft cocktail events. He is the owner of the Bee's Knees Bar Services, a hospitality consulting firm that provides restaurant and bar consultation, private event bar services, staff training, brand ambassadorship, and other corporate event and consulting services. He is the President of the Manitoba Bartender's Guild, a collaborative community group that fosters education and networking among industry professionals. He has travelled North America representing Canada for hospitality industry bar events such as Camp Runamok, Tiki by the Sea, Behind the Barrel, Bar Institute, and Tales of the Cocktail.

KENTUCKY UNICORN**

1 ½ oz (45 ml) bourbon whiskey (Bulleit)
¾ oz (22.5 ml) Cynar
1 barspoon Roast peach syrup (p. 204)
2 dash Peychaud's bitters

Glass: Old-Fashioned / Rocks
Method: Stir all ingredients with ice and strain over fresh ice
Garnish: Lemon twist and fresh peach slice

NICOLE COTE

Nicole Cote is a bartender born and raised in Winnipeg. Like most folks from the prairies, she is creative and resourceful. Her style tends to focus on both sustainability —with a focus on local ingredients—and accessibility. Essentially, a contemporary classic approach.

After completing the 2018 class of the Cocktail Apprentice Program at Tales of the Cocktail, her next goal is bartending internationally. In her spare time, she focuses on painting, collage, internet deep dives, and hanging out with her cat, Peychaud.

CLEVER VISUAL METAPHOR**

1 oz (30 ml) bourbon (Buffalo Trace)
¾ oz (22.5 ml) Ramazzotti
¼ oz (7.5 ml) Fernet-Branca
¼ oz (7.5 ml) Grenadine (p. 197)
1 barspoon Islay Scotch

Glass: Small Cocktail / Nick & Nora
Method: Stir all ingredients with ice and strain
Garnish: Lemon twist

CHRIS HOWELL

Chris' bartending career began, as do many others, slinging highballs, pouring draft beer, and (exclusively) shaking Martinis. This all changed after his introduction to The Bar Book by Jeffrey Morgenthaler and Death and Co.: Modern Classic Cocktails by Alex Day, David Kaplan and Nick Fauchald. These tomes inspired him to delve deeper into the world of cocktails and to develop relationships with inspiring people who became his mentors and fellow tenders of the bar. This spark developed into a creative passion that ran rampant and has travelled with him from Vancouver to Ottawa and now to Winnipeg.

The main lessons he has learnt in his years behind the bar are not to be afraid to experiment or fail; being precise and consistent with all drinks; be open to new information from peers or guests; and finally seize all the opportunities that this industry extends, because you never know where it'll lead. This field of work comes with a great community, an extensive history and a lot of trial and error—but it is ever worth it.

TRAVEL BUDDY*

1 oz (30 ml) American rye whiskey (Knob Creek Rye)
½ oz (15 ml) Aperol
½ oz (15 ml) Lillet Blanc
1 barspoon Fernet-Branca
1-2 dashes Regans' Orange Bitters No. 6

Glass: Small Cocktail / Nick & Nora
Method: Stir all ingredients with ice and strain
Garnish: Lemon twist and discard

JOSEY KRAHN

Growing up in Winnipeg, Josey had the advantage of being from a deeply rooted, tight-knit community that is somewhat isolated from the trends of the bigger Canadian cities. People in the creative communities look inward to form their crafts, and this cocktail scene is no different. Coming up in hospitality, working in beer joints and music halls, the artists and musicians that frequent these places have played a huge role in forming Josey's approach to cocktails which is defined largely by authenticity and simplicity.

The chefs, fellow bartenders, and impresarios that she has had the opportunity to work with and around have helped her to develop an affinity for cocktails that have few ingredients and focus on balance and simplicity. Josey loves to think that her drinks can be made by anyone who has the inclination to care for ingredients and the intention of execution.

THE RED RIVER SHOPPING CART*

¾ oz (22.5 ml) gin
(Plymouth Navy Strength)
¾ oz (22.5 ml) Campari
¾ oz (22.5 ml) lime juice
½ oz (15 ml) Simple syrup
(p.209)
1 ½ oz (45 ml) IPA

Glass: Old-Fashioned /
Rocks
Method: Shake all
ingredients except IPA with
ice and strain over a large ice
cube, top with IPA
Garnish: Grapefruit twist

SHELBY LINDEN

Shelby is a lover of strong bourbon, bitter coffee, and long walks in mild temperatures. She was born and raised in Youngstown, Ohio, and moved to Winnipeg at age 17 to start a new life with her mother and Italian stepfamily. She fell in love with Canada and plans to live in Winnipeg for the rest of her life. Winnipeg is viewed as being the underdog rising of Canada, but it feels like home to her.

She started bartending because she wanted to make delicious drinks for herself without leaving the house, and after getting the hang of the craft she switched careers from visual merchandising to bartending fulltime. She has now been in the industry for three years. When she isn't bartending, she volunteers at Main Street Project, a non-profit that provides a place of safety, support, and shelter for vulnerable Winnipeg citizens.

AMERICAN WOMAN**

2 oz (60 ml) bourbon (Woodford Reserve)
1 oz (30 ml) lemon juice
1 oz (30 ml) Honey cinnamon syrup (p. 198)
1 oz (30 ml) egg white
2 dashes Fee Brothers Black Walnut Bitters

Glass: Highball / Collins
Method: Dry shake all ingredients then wet shake with ice. Strain over fresh ice and top with sparkling water
Garnish: Freshly cracked pepper

ELSA TAYLOR

Elsa Taylor is a six-year veteran bartender from Winnipeg who worked in restaurants throughout high school and weaselled her way behind the bar. In 2015, she opened a bar called The Roost on Corydon, which she co-owns with partners Caiden Bircham and Ike Hedenstierna. Since then, Elsa has written and executed a different cocktail menu for each season, resulting in hundreds of new recipes. Her interests outside of work include poetry, music, feminism, and queer theory.

DEATH FOR BREAKFAST***

1 ½ oz (45 ml) amber rum
½ oz (15 ml) absinthe
2/3 oz (20 ml) Froot Loop orgeat (p. 195)
1 oz (30 ml) orange juice
½ oz (15 ml) lime juice
4 dashes Angostura bitters
Top with sparkling wine

Glass: Small Cereal Bowl
Method: Fill your bowl with crushed ice, add all ingredients except absinthe. Stir with spoon to mix
Garnish: Hollowed out orange end in the centre of drink, then arrange mint leaves around it, and sprinkle Fruit Loops

around the edges of the bowl. Leave the spoon in and add a straw. Pour absinthe into the orange and light on fire.

ERIK THORDARSON

Ten years ago, Erik was dishwashing at The Keg when he transitioned to serving for the following two years. He then began work in a local pub, where he was thrown behind the bar. An older gentleman ordered a Dry Gin Martini from him, straight up with olives. He had a basic understanding of what he wanted and attempted to piece it together. The man said it was "okay", but Erik wondered to himself would he be happy if this was served to him.

He has kept this philosophy throughout his entire bartending career; ensuring that every single product that hits the table is up to the highest standard. He now owns and operates his own restaurant and cocktail bar, Sous Sol, located in the Osborne Village. The feel of the place is to have fun with drinks and don't take things too seriously. It's probably why the team gravitates towards the relaxed nature of tiki cocktails.

THE OLD PORT*

1oz (30 ml) aged rum (Ron Matusalem Gran Reserva)
¾ oz (22.5 ml) sweet vermouth (Punt e Mes)
¼ oz (7.5 ml) crème de cassis
¼ oz (7.5 ml) Islay whisky (Ardbeg 10 year)
2 dashes of Fee Brothers Black Walnut Bitters

Glass: Snifter
Method: Stir all ingredients with ice and strain
Garnish: None

QUEBEC

QUEBEC is the country's French province, rich in history and ferociously untouched from the Anglo influence of the rest of Canada. Quebec is an essential part of French history—it was the place of French immigrants' entry into the new world of North America. Two major cities represent the province, Quebec City and Montréal, and both represent old world and new world France respectively. The people of Quebec are ferociously patriotic to their heritage, many only speaking French and identifying as such. This gives the province its uniqueness: Visiting Quebec is like travelling all the way to the French countryside— beautiful, passionate, and wonderfully unique in its eccentricities.

128

QUEBEC CITY

IF YOU WANT to experience Europe without escaping North America, Quebec City is where you'll get it—it's rooted in rich French history and left almost untouched by English impression. Craft breweries make classic French- and Belgian-style beers which have been popular for over a decade. And recently, distilleries have led to the burgeoning cocktail culture.

With industry icons like Patrice Plante (aka Mr. Cocktail) and Patrick Beaulieu of Hono Izakaya leading the charge, Quebec City's francophone bartenders are rising to rival those of their sister city, Montréal. This small community is giving themselves a voice that everyone can hear. Or drink.—Kevin Demers

JEAN-FÉLIX DESFOSSÉS

Hospitality and creativity are what triggered Jean-Felix's passion for this beautiful profession, that he's been working in for six years. Desfossés originally started as a bartender for the Fairmont Château Frontenac in Quebec City and ended up in charge of the bar program there after three years. He has now left Château Frontenac to work on new project Truffles On The Rocks, creating food-and-cocktail oriented content for social media with his partner.

Truffles on The Rocks combines the sense of community and creativity that he loves so much about bartending but in a different way. They get to meet, create, and work with many people all the time: People that share the same passion for food and beverage from around the world.

DILL WITH IT!*

2 oz (60 ml) Tanqueray Rangpur
¾ oz (22.5 ml) Suze
2 sprigs fresh dill
2 dashes Bittered Sling Cascade Celery Bitters

Glass: Small Cocktail / Nick & Nora
Method: Stir all ingredients with ice and strain
Garnish: Dill sprig

MAXIME ST-GERMAIN

Maxime started bartending at his parent's golf club in 2006 when he was 18 years old, and used bartending as a side hustle while studying to become a kinesiologist at university. Even after university, he used to be a personal trainer on weekdays and work in bars on the weekends. This all changed in 2015 when he quit personal training and got hired as a fulltime bartender at Le Shaker and at Le Bureau de Poste at the same time. This is where he met Marc-André Fillion and Julien Vézina, two mentors who inspired him to creatine amazing cocktails and make customers feel as if they were in their own home.

They brought him to a few events and cocktail contests, where he solidified his love with cocktails. This lead to him to attend every contest or event possible. After a few years of working various bar positions, he was lucky enough to open his own cocktail bar, Chez Tao!, in December 2017 and while he may no longer be there, he is always happy with his work in the industry.

GREMLINE*

1 ½ oz (45 ml) blanco
tequila (Patrón)
1 oz (30 ml) fresh
pineapple juice
½ oz (15 ml) tamarind
paste
½ oz (15 ml) agave syrup
¼ oz (7.5 ml) lime juice
90g ice

Glass: Large Cocktail
Method: Blend with ice
and pour
Garnish: Dehydrated
lime wheel

JULIEN VÉZINA

Born and raised in Quebec City, Julien has been bartending since 2013, when Mike Boisvert from Le Bureau de Poste gave him his first opportunity to jump behind the bar. His passion for the industry was ignited by competing in a couple of competitions, and he most notably made it to the national final for the Best Caesar in Town national two years in a row.

Then Julien began networking and meeting mentors, new friends, and connections such as JP D'Auteuil, who was the Rémy Martin brand ambassador at the time, and Patrice Plante, who later became a friend and now partner in the industry. After working Le Bistro L'Atelier, he then opened Honō Izakaya in Quebec City with his three partners Ariane Boudreau, Patrick Beaulieu and Thomas Casault.

AKI**

1 ½ oz (45 ml) cognac
(Hennessy VS)
1oz (30 ml) shiso umeshu
½ oz (15 ml) Vanilla shrub
(p. 209)
¼ oz (7.5 ml) Rice orgeat
(p. 203)
1 dash cardamom bitters

Glass: Small Cocktail /
Nick & Nora
Method: Shake all
ingredients with ice and
double strain
Garnish: Shiso leaf

MONTRÉAL

MONTRÉAL is a small city, a big town, known as the place to eat well with some world-renowned venues on the ever-growing restaurant scene such as Joe Beef, Pied Cochon, Garde Manger, and Maison Public showcasing the city's culinary culture. With these stalwart restaurants overshadowing the industry, the cocktail scene is now starting to emerge with some amazing innovation, creativity, and hospitality.

The trend started in the early 2000s with cocktail bars like Le Lab and Distillery setting the tone. In 2016, most of the disciples of both Fabian Mallard at Le Lab Comptoir and Phil Hamman at Le Distillerie began stepping out on their own and opening their own cocktail bars. Now in 2019, world-class level cocktail bars with fantastic service are appearing and beginning to gather accolades, just like their culinary brethren.

Montréal is a multicultural city that has always been known for great food, beautiful architecture, and above all the feeling of European joie de vivre. But, with some passionate people at the helm, Montréal's cocktail scene will definitely be added to that list.—Kevin Demers

ÉMILE ARCHAMBAULT

While only 25 years old, Émile has been in the restaurant industry for 11 years. He took his first bartending job five years ago at a bar in the Old Port of Montréal. Luckily, the management saw potential in him and gave him carte blanche on the cocktail menu, allowing him the freedom to build his creativity through working with the kitchen and exploring new flavors.

After a few years, Antonin Mousseau-Rivard of Le Mousso approached him to come on board for the opening of the restaurant, combining a world-class menu with paired cocktails. Le Mousso opened Émile's eyes to a world of possibility, utilizing the various culinary machines at his disposal and working closely with the kitchen to discover new flavors and aromas, which only built his confidence in his creativity. In 2018, he made the finals of the Made with Booze competition for the second year in a row and received a nomination for Best Bartender in Quebec at Gala des Lauriers de la Gastronomie in 2019.

GOLDENCAP***

1 oz (30 ml) gin (Barhill)
¾ oz (22.5 ml) port
1 oz (30 ml) Mushroom and corn syrup (p. 201)
¾ oz (22.5 ml) lemon juice
6 drops espresso coffee

Glass: Old-Fashioned / Rocks
Method: Shake all ingredients with ice and double stain over fresh ice
Garnish: Torched porcini powder

MAXIME BOIVIN

Currently holding court at Bar George, Max has been able to apply his skills to some great venues including co-owning the Midway Tavern. His favorite place to enjoy making a cocktail is at home with some friends and a BBQ—just like food, cocktails must be consumed while surrounded by people you love. For the last decade he has traversed from the Old Port of Montréal to the Plateau, where people come to fill themselves with love, friends and Last Words.

SPRING HAS SPRUNG*

1 oz (30 ml) gin (KM12)
½ oz (15 ml) Amermelade
½ oz (15 ml) lemon juice
2 dashes Bittered Sling Grapefruit & Hop Bitters
3 oz (90 ml) 1642 Tonic Water

Glass: Old-Fashioned / Rocks
Method: Shake all ingredients except tonic with ice and strain over ice. Top with tonic
Garnish: Grapefruit chip and rosemary sprig

KATE BOUSHEL

After leaving the restaurant and bar industry for a career in government and public relations for nearly a decade, Kate's passion for local flavours, spirits and cocktails as well as her natural inclination towards the art of hospitality brought her back to bartending. Since her return to the industry, she has had the pleasure of working with and learning from some of the best bartenders in Canada while working the wood at notable Montréal bars such as Le Mal Necessaire and the Atwater Cocktail Club. She has also competed on a global and national scale for industry competitions such as Marie Brizard Masters, Diageo World Class, Bombay Sapphire's Most Imaginative Bartender, and Speed Rack. In 2017, her cocktail, The Dominion, was named Canada's "Next Great Cocktail" by *enRoute* Magazine.

Resourceful and creative, she has since managed to combine her past experiences and academic achievements with her passion for the bar by creating her position as beverage and education director with the Barroco Group, which includes the Atwater Cocktail Club, Milky Way Cocktail Bar, and many other restaurants. Along with her work, she strives to give back and help build a stronger and healthier community through mentoring, fundraising, and knowledge-sharing.

BEYOND SMOKE & MIRRORS*

1 oz (30 ml) reposado tequila (Don Julio)
1 oz (30 ml) manzanilla sherry (La Guitana)
½ oz (15 ml) Cocchi Americano
½ oz (15 ml) Cocchi Rosa
1 dash Scrappy's Lavender Bitters
2 dashes Bittered Sling Cascade Celery bitters
2 dashes Bittered Sling Lem-Marrakech bitters

Glass: Small Cocktail / Nick & Nora
Method: Throw cocktail with ice
Garnish: None

MAX COUBES

Max has been in the world of hospitality for over 15 years as a founding member and co-owner of Le 4e Mur, a speakeasy in the heart of Montréal. He has become a driver in Montréal's hospitality scene through various initiatives. Utilising his training in visual communication, he puts his skills into practice in order to create inspiring graphic worlds that encompass his love of cocktails and spirits through his work with 1ou2cocktails.com, a website with the purpose of spreading the cocktail love for the general public.

NO TUXEDO*

1 ½ oz (45 ml) old Tom gin (Cirka 375)
¼ oz (7.5 ml) oloroso sherry
¼ oz (7.5 ml) manzanilla sherry
½ oz (15 ml) Suze
2 barspoons Yellow Chartreuse
2 dashes Chamomile tincture (p. 191)
2 dashes Bittered Sling Celery Bitters

Glass: Small Cocktail / Nick & Nora
Method: Stir all ingredients with ice and strain
Garnish: Lemon twist and discard

DRAHOS CHYTRY

Drahos was born in communist Czechoslovakia and came to Canada at the age of nine. Growing up, he aspired to bartend. And as soon as he hit age 18, he started bartending classes and working right away in the back bar of the kitchen at Mother Tucker's restaurant. He always viewed bartending as a long-term career and has spent the last 23 years behind the bar at Club Med, Hotel W, pubs, clubs, and music festivals like Osheaga, hundreds of fundraisers, Grand Prix, Bar George, and now at the prestigious Four Seasons Hotel. Bartending has afforded him some amazing trips like Absolut Vodka which sent him to Sweden and travelling to Peru for a month in the name of the Pisco Sour.

THAITINI*

1 oz (30 ml) vanilla vodka (Absolut)
1 oz (30 ml) Chambord
2 oz (60 ml) fresh pineapple juice
2 basil leaves
2 ginger root discs

Glass: Large Cocktail
Method: Muddle ginger in shaker, add all ingredients, shake with ice and double strain
Garnish: Basil leaf, 2 blackberries and dusting of vanilla powder

ANDRE DUNCAN

Andre began his career in a stereotypical way, working as a server to pay for tuition in university. But he quickly realised that this industry was his calling. While he enjoyed working the floor, the mystique of the bar fascinated him and drew him into buying into his first bar, the late Well's Pub in Sherbrooke. His time at Well's was tumultuous, but it sparked his interest in cocktails, pushing him to buy and research cocktail books which fueled his artistic side.

A short stint at L'Assommoir Notre-Dame in Montréal, working for free behind the bar to learn as much as possible led him to travel to Australia for a working holiday. He ended up in Sydney and working as a barback in The Baxter Inn, one of the best bars in the world. After this short tenure, he travelled the country, working in pubs, dive boats, and enjoying the traditional activities of a backpacker before leaving for an eight-month trip across Southeast Asia to discover new flavours and inspiration.

When he came back to Quebec in 2015, he set himself a clear objective: He wanted to create a cocktail scene in his hometown. What was meant to be a challenge quickly became an obsession. In 2017, he won Auchentoshan's New Malt Order national competition and headed to Glasgow to blend the Bartender's Blend. He went on to become the World Champion of Jameson's Barrelmen's Homecoming in Ireland. All he knows is that fortune favours the bold, so he'll keep being the boldest.

PAUL WALKER*

2 oz (60 ml) rye whiskey (High West Rendezvous)
¼ oz (7.5 ml) crème de cacao
¼ oz (7.5 ml) maraschino (Luxardo)
¼ oz (7.5 ml) Simple syrup (p.209)
2 dashes Fee Brothers Aztec Chocolate Bitters
2 dashes Fee Brothers Cherry Bitters

Glass: Old-Fashioned / Rocks
Method: Stir all ingredients with ice and strain over large cube
Garnish: Orange twist and cherry

JONATHAN HOMIER

Jonathan got his first spark for bartending while studying restaurant management at ITHQ in Montréal at the tender age of 17. He realized that bartending was the perfect balance between being a cook and a waiter. He enjoyed the creative and manual side of a cook's job but he couldn't picture himself without the human connection of a guest. After graduation, Jonathan started as a busboy in one of Montréal's first bars with a real cocktail program, La Distillerie, which turned out to be the best training ground for him. He then went on to get his first bar job at Le Lab, Comptoir à Cocktails. It was only there that he realized the infinite potential of the bartending profession.

In the next few years, Jonathan gained experience in a wide range of establishments, from nightclub to five-star hotel bar. During that time, he also began competing in numerous bartending competitions, and won the 2012 Appleton Estate Bartenders Challenge representing Canada at the world finals. He is now bar manager at Montréal's Perles & Paddock.

WINTER COFFEE EH!**

1 ½ oz (45 ml) Canadian
Whisky (Lot 40)
¾ oz (22.5 ml) Lapsang
souchong maple syrup
(p. 198)
3 oz (90 ml) rich black coffee
Float of heavy cream
Mist of Gourmet Sauvage
sweet clover extract

Glass: Special Coffee Mug
Method: Build in heated
glass, float cream
Garnish: None

NABIL BEN EL KHATTAB

Moroccan-born Nabil Ben el Khattab started working in the industry in 2006 and has travelled the world from Lyon, France to Japan. In his travels, he became very interested in Mediterranean flavors when he arrived in Montréal in 2015 and began to explore and apply them to his position as head bartender at the Fairmont of Queen Elizabeth. The Casablanca native hopes to open his own cocktail bar in the future. But in the meantime, he is enjoying participation in competitions such as Diageo World Class and Bacardi Legacy.

BROOKLYN NO:2**

¾ oz (22.5 ml) mezcal (Alipus)
1 oz (30 ml) rye whisky (Lot 40)
1 oz (30 ml) dry vermouth (Dolin)
¼ oz (7.5 ml) Amaro Monténégro
1 barspoon Chinotto liqueur
2 dashes Peychaud's Whiskey Barrel-Aged bitters
2 dashes Angostura bitters

Glass: Small Cocktail / Nick & Nora
Method: Stir all ingredients with ice and strain
Garnish: Orange and lemon twist and discard, finish with cherry

SAM KIRK

Hailing from Australia, Sam cut his teeth in the dives and nefarious drinking houses of East London. His time involved moonlighting as a bathtub gin distiller and part-time chemist. Returning triumphantly home to Sydney, Sam felt that a spell of bartending was in order. He then learnt the most important lessons in bartending: How to make a pun for every cocktail name, and how to make 15 Espresso Martinis in one go. After being home a spell, Sam decided he wanted the world, adventure, and to see what it's like to make a cocktail in the frigid winters of Montréal. You can find him in the depths of the Coldroom, since early 2017, churning out all sorts of wild libations.

THE DOVE**

1 ½ oz (45 ml) mezcal (Convite)
1 ½ oz (45 ml) Acidified pink grapefruit (p. 190)
½ oz (15 ml) Rosemary syrup (p. 205)
¾ oz (22.5 ml) egg white
1 barspoon avocado oil

Glass: Large Cocktail
Method: Shake all ingredients with ice, dry shake and double strain
Garnish: Rosemary sprig

ARNAUD LEDUC

Arnaud left the construction sector six years ago, and has been working in dive bars pouring pints and shots ever since. Now 27 years old, he has taken that grounding in dive bars and is applying it to his newfound passion for cocktails, spirits, and attention to flavours. The obvious next step was to start competing in competitions including Bacardi Legacy, Patrón Perfectionists, and Diageo World Class.

Arnaud now revels in meeting new industry people, researching, and teaching folk about the things that he loves, especially his fascination with fortified wine and mezcal and the way that they play together in cocktails. His cocktails reflect his personal style and his growing passion for the hospitality industry.

LE MANOEUVRE*

1 ½ oz (45 ml) sweet vermouth (Punt e Mes)
¾ oz (22.5 ml) mezcal (Fidencio Espadin Joven)
¾ oz (22.5 ml) elderflower liqueur (St. Germain)
¼ oz (7.5 ml) amontillado sherry
2 dashes Bittered Sling Malagasy Chocolate

Glass: Small Cocktail / Nick & Nora
Method: Stir all ingredients with ice and strain
Garnish: Orange twist

EMILIE LOISELLE

A 10-year veteran of the Montréal bartending scene, Emilie has worked in some of the city's finest establishments, most recently working as the manager of the Cloakroom Bar. She boasts a large arsenal of technical and creative skills, and over the last few years she has had the chance to showcase these in many competitions, including as a National Finalist at the 2017, 2018, and 2019 Diageo World Class and Speed Rack competitions.

Throughout her experience with cocktails she has developed a style that is very direct and focuses on unexpected and interesting flavour combinations that concentrate on the liquid in the glass over the peripherals. Discovering the tradition of drinking Italian liqueurs with olives while travelling in Italy in 2016 inspired her to create her signature cocktail, Dirty Martini #2—a simple but complex libation in all aspects.

DIRTY MARTINI #2*

2 oz (60 ml) London dry gin (Tanqueray)
1 oz (30 ml) rosé vermouth (Cocchi Rosa)
¼ oz (7.5 ml) olive brine

Glass: Small Cocktail / Nick & Nora
Method: Stir all ingredients with ice and strain
Garnish: Olive, twist, or whatever your heart desires

SABRINA MAILHOT

Sabrina was born on the south shore of Montréal Island but moved with her mom to Victoriaville when she was a few weeks old. Always living as a sort of nomad, she grew up admiring her mother's strength. This laid the foundation for her career in restaurants, originally as a way to provide for herself like her mother and grandmother, but then turning it into something more.

It was here that the ambient sound of the voices, of dishwashers running, plates and glasses being served, always felt like home. It was more a question of habit back then—washing dishes and clearing tables were not a passion. Art was. Painting and drawing, music and movies, she aspired to be an artist, a musician, picturing herself even acting. But then as she progressed in the industry, Montréal showed her a way to merge her many passions with working behind the bar. This is where her career as a bartender flourished, fed by the drive and hard work of her many mentors and whole community. She is grateful for the opportunities that the industry has lent to her in her career, and continues to pursue her passion.

SÉQUITO*

2 oz (60 ml) aged rum
(Bacardi Ocho)
1 oz (30 ml) orange juice
½ oz (15 ml) lime juice
½ oz (15 ml) grenadine
¼ oz (7.5 ml) banana
liqueur

Glass: Large Cocktail
Method: Shake all
ingredients with ice and
double strain
Garnish: Lime wheel

FABIEN MALLIARD

Fabien has been in the bar world for over 25 years, including being at the helm of Mixoart Entertainment, which boasts notable ventures like Le Lab and Comptoir à Cocktails in its stable. Maillard is one of the first pioneers of the modern cocktail culture in Montréal and Quebec, showcasing the talents of the province and winning cocktail and flair competitions the world over while contributing to the development of talents in the Montréal cocktail scene.

MAI CLARIFIED GOAT MILK TAI***

66 oz (1950 ml) goats' milk
33 oz (975 ml) orgeat syrup (The Lab)
33 oz (975 ml) lime juice
33 oz (975 ml) pineapple juice
16.5 oz (490 ml) Pierre Ferrand Dry Curaçao
16.5 oz (490 ml) Plantation O.F.T.D Rum
33 oz (975 ml) Plantation Original Dark Rum

Glass: Old-Fashioned / Rocks
Batch Method: Batch all ingredients except goats' milk. Bring the goats' milk to a simmer and add to batch. Let stand for 24 hours in the fridge. Carefully filter through grease cones of coffee filters. Bottle and refrigerate
Single Method: Pour 2 oz (60 ml) over large ice cube
Garnish: Mint sprig

PIERRE HUGUES MAROIS

Pierre is the beverage director for the Coldroom and El Pequino group in Montréal. He is an eight-year veteran of the industry after leaving the graphic design business and focusing on bartending as a career. His first job was at Montréal's cocktail institution, La Distillerie, where he had tenure for three years, meeting mentors to develop his technical style, knowledge, and guest service technique. He went on to manage Midway bar for three years and gained a deeper understanding of cocktail culture. Then he began to compete in cocktail competitions.

Coldroom and El Pequino are his main focus, but he still has the opportunity to be an educator for the Quebec Alcohol Corporation and write the cocktail section for *Umami Magazine*. On the side, he still likes to practice his design and art.

THE MIST***

1 ¼ oz (37.5 ml) gin (Sipsmith)
½ oz (15 ml) aged grappa
¼ oz (7.5 ml) manzanilla
sherry (La Gitana)
1 oz (30 ml) Clarified pear &
green pea syrup (p. 193)
1 oz (30 ml) Citric water
(p. 193)

Glass: Highball / Collins
Method: Shake all ingredients
with ice and double strain over
fresh ice, top with soda
Garnish: Dehydrated pear

SEAN MICHAEL MCCAFFREY

Born and raised in a small farming town called Ormstown in Quebec, Sean moved to Montréal in 2007 and started working in a pub right away. He eventually moved on to fine dining venues at Le Bremner and Le Garde Manger. After a few years working his way up the ladder in The Crown Salts family (owners of Le Bremner and Le Garde Manger) he left to help open up a new pub, Bishop & Bagg, which was the second pub in the Burgundy Lion group. After five great years as general manager of Bishop & Bagg, Sean joined the group as a partner for its latest venture in Old Montréal called The Wolf & Workman Free House.

THE BITTER BLEND*

½ oz (15 ml) gin (Dandy)
½ oz (15 ml) bourbon (Bulleit)
½ oz (15 ml) Cynar
½ oz (15 ml) Campari
1 oz (30 ml) sweet vermouth (Carpano Antica Formula)

Glass: Old-Fashioned / Rocks
Method: Stir all ingredients with ice and strain over fresh ice
Garnish: Orange twist

ASILEX RODRIGUEZ

Just a few years ago, Asilex Rodriguez was bored to death behind a modest bar in the Village, over in the south-eastern end of downtown Montréal. Day in and day out, she saw the same clients coming in to chat over a beer. She wanted more. Someone told her: "If you want to be a bartender, that is perfectly fine, but don't settle for being just an average bartender. Aim to be one of the best in the city, and then the world."

So Asilex decided to take her passion to the next level and see how far she could go. She got a gig at Philémon, a wine bar in Old Montréal where she began to learn her craft, the art of wine service, and all the attention to minute detail the latter requires. Her passion for mixology knew no depths, and she landed a job at Le Lab, a cocktail bar and one of the first speakeasies in Montréal, studying under some of Montréal's finest and even learning some classic flair for good measure. She now can be found managing Bar Datcha/ Kabinet in the Mile-End and working at Bootlegger L'Authentique every Thursday for LeCypher—a funk, soul and hip-hop open jam night.

ACV (ABSINTHE/CHARTREUSE/VODKA)**

1 ½ oz (45 ml) vodka (Stolichnaya)
½ oz (15 ml) Green Chartreuse
1 ½ oz (45 ml) fresh lime juice
1 oz (30 ml) Ginger syrup (p. 196)
½ oz (15 ml) water
2 dashes Angostura
2 dashes Peychaud's bitters
2 or 3 slices of candied ginger
1/4 oz (7.5 ml) absinthe

Glass: Absinthe glass
Method: Combine all ingredients except absinthe in a saucepan and gently heat. Pour ingredients into absinthe glass and gently layer absinthe on top.
Garnish: Ginger disc

MEGAN TURCOTTE

Megan was 19 when she finished cooking school and dived into the restaurant industry. She worked in Montréal and abroad for about seven years in the back of house before an opening in the front appeared to her. She worked for a year as a waitress and bartender before applying to Burgundy Lion, where she is now head bartender. She found that cocktails bridged the gap in her kitchen experience and the bar, combining flavors and learning about unknown spirits. The new learning experience and the ability to connect directly with customers is what made her love bartending so much, using all the great products that Quebec has to offer into a singular drinking experience.

SCOTTISH REVIVAL**

1oz (30 ml) gin (The Botanist)
½ oz (15 ml) Galliano
½ oz (15 ml) De la Copa Vermouth
½ oz (15 ml) lemon juice
½ oz (15 ml) Québec honey syrup
½ oz (15 ml) crowberry tea
Atomizer Tamdhu 10

Glass: Small Cocktail / Nick & Nora
Method: Stir all ingredients with ice and strain
Garnish: None

150

SAM TURP

With a Francophone father and an Anglophone mother, Sam has Irish and Scottish heritage, as well as an indigenous background. Both of his parents are in the visual arts, are intellectual, and well educated, which means that he stands out as the black sheep in the family. He never considered the hospitality industry as a career, but after the last 10 years he has been learning and progressing to land in one of Montréal's very best restaurants, Le Garde Manger. Progressing from bartender to bar manager and now taking on even more of a management role, he has grown with the company and plans to continue doing so.

APERITIVO COCKTAIL*

¾ oz (22.5 ml) Averna Amaro
¾ oz (22.5 ml) Aperol
½ oz (15 ml) Lillet Blanc
½ oz (15 ml) sweet vermouth
½ oz (15 ml) lemon juice

Glass: Old-Fashioned / Rocks
Method: Shake all ingredients with ice and double strain over fresh ice
Garnish: Lemon wheel

THOMAS YEO

Thomas Yeo was born in Chelsea, Quebec and grew up on the Ontario/Quebec border. He completed a history undergraduate degree in Montréal while getting his first taste of the hospitality industry, working part-time at an Italian restaurant. He moved to South Africa for his last semester before embarking on a bit of a world tour, spending five months in southern Africa, South East Asia, and western Europe. During his travels he realized that he hadn't explored his own country and made the move to Halifax to enrol in his masters and see what the east coast had to offer.

It was in Halifax that he started to develop and explore his passion for food and drink, first through cooking and later through cocktails, when he helped to build and expand a tiki program at a local restaurant. Realizing that hospitality and cocktails were his true calling, he decided that it would be foolish to forego a career he loved simply because he had invested time and money in a degree he no longer wanted to use. The less-secure path can be daunting, but diving into hospitality headfirst opened up endless possibilities. After making it to the 2018 Diageo World Class national finals he moved to more elevated cocktail programs at Halifax cocktail mainstays Highwayman and Fieldguide. While working there he qualified for the 2019 Bacardi Legacy and made the national finals, before moving to Montréal to take his bartending to the next level. Today you can find him managing the Atwater Cocktail Club and preparing for his second crack at the World Class national finals.

SAZÓN**

1 ½ oz (45 ml) blanco tequila (Don Julio)
½ oz (15 ml) Cuixe mezcal (El Jolgorio)
½ oz (15 ml) Ancho Reyez
¾ oz (22.5 ml) Tomatillo pulp and cilantro root cordial (p. 208)
¾ oz (22.5 ml) Acidified tomatillo juice (p. 190)
2 dashes Bittered Sling Celery Bitters

Glass: Steep-sided Wooden Bowl
Method: Shake all ingredients with ice and strain, pack with crushed ice and insert metal straw
Garnish: Dehydrated tomatillo chips, inverted tomatillo husk and cilantro

ONTARIO

ONTARIO is the most populated province in the country, containing almost 40 percent of Canada's residents. The province borders the Great Lakes, and has some of Canada's most well-known attractions, including the Niagara Falls. It boasts Ottawa and Toronto as its major cities: Ottawa is the nation's political centre; while Toronto is its largest city, a rich and diverse metropolis where all cultures are accepted, and different communities have carved out their own spaces and neighbourhoods to create their own little piece of home.

TORONTO

TORONTO is the capital of Ontario and the most populous city in Canada. It stands to reason then that there are more cocktail bars in Toronto per capita than anywhere else in the country.

In the late 2000s, The Harbord Room, The Black Hoof, and BarChef all opened, giving Torontonians the opportunity to dive into classic cocktails, new takes on classic recipes, and even molecular extrapolations. The drive to make better drinks and increase guest experience spread throughout places like The Drake Hotel and Brassaii. Many staff members from those spots went on to open and manage many of the other well-known cocktail-serving establishments in the city.

Toronto is now in what some call in its fourth wave of cocktail enthusiasts and bars. There is a great place to grab a cocktail in every neighbourhood in the city, so you're never too far from exactly what you want.—Jessica Blaine Smith and Josh Lindley

JAMES BAILEY

James' roots in the industry began when he worked as a sommelier at his brother's French restaurant, Celestin. In this role, he was fascinated by the idea of being able to enhance a guest's experience through a perfect pairing. It was with this concept in mind that he gained a newfound appreciation for making cocktails. By being able to create a custom-made libation for a guest, he has been able to capture a completely unique experience that wine sometimes cannot produce. After delving into the world of bartending, he focused his passions on infusing the Spanish and Peruvian flavors that he grew up with into crafting cocktails. Through bartending, he has been able to co-own two Peruvian-inspired restaurants, was awarded Ontario Hostelry Institutes's Top 30 under 30, and represented Canada at Bombay Sapphire's Most Imaginative Bartender competition in 2018.

LA PACHAMAMA**

1 ½ oz (45 ml) pisco (La Caravedo Torontel)
½ oz (15 ml) cachaça (Novo Fogo Silver)
¾ oz (22.5 ml) lime juice
¾ oz (22.5 ml) Cucumber fennel cordial (p. 194)
3 tarragon leaves
¾ oz (22.5 ml) egg white

Glass: Large Cocktail
Method: Shake all ingredients with ice, then dry shake and double strain
Garnish: Drops of Angostura bitters

JOHN BUNNER

John's noble calling of looking after his guests began seven years ago at Toronto Temperance Society. Following stints there and at and Yours Truly, in 2015, he opened and managed Alo restaurant's barroom. He directed the bar programs at Aloette and Alobar Yorkville restaurants. At present, he is the operations director at the Alo Food Group.

ARRÊTE DE FUMER!*

2 oz (60 ml) dry vermouth (Noilly Prat)
¾ oz (22.5 ml) Islay whisky (Laphroaig Quarter Cask)
1/3 oz (10 ml) Drambuie
7 drops Coster's Black Tea & Wormwood Bitters

Glass: Small Cocktail / Nick & Nora
Method: Stir all ingredients with ice and strain
Garnish: Lemon twist

IN FOCUS

JOSH LINDLEY
& JESSICA BLAINE SMITH
BARTENDER ATLAS

Photographer Jessica Blaine Smith and bartender Josh Lindley launched Bartender Atlas in May 2016. The idea for it was first sparked a year earlier while on their honeymoon in Australia where they encountered the best service, skill, and attitude from some of the least-known bartenders in the world. There are many places to find out about best bars, award-winning cocktails, and industry leaders, but what about the people making those drinks night in and night out?

In basic terms, Bartender Atlas is a worldwide directory of bartenders—there are bartenders from literally every corner of the globe listed on the site. Drink slingers the world over fill out a short questionnaire that includes things like where they are from; what drinks they like to drink; what they collect; and where they took their last vacation. The intent is to have the general public understand that being a bartender is more than just putting things in a glass. These are real people that may have similar interests, and it is highly encouraged that a reader settle in on a stool in front of one of them, start conversation, and enjoy a cocktail or two.

Besides running the website, Jess and Josh also put together several events such as competitions and spirit classes both for Bartender Atlas and other brands. Annually, Bartender Atlas organizes three days of events in a different city which are dubbed "tours". These tours include cocktail competitions, guest spots, and bar hops as well as daytime events such as brunches, pilates classes, and basketball games. So far Toronto, Melbourne, and Halifax have been included on these tours. For each tour, a guest bartender from another city (or country) is flown in to participate in the events and for the opportunity for everyone to learn from one another about different markets. These tours are open to both industry folk as well as regular cocktail enthusiasts. The goal with every event that Bartender Atlas organizes is to build a more united community amongst bartenders by introducing them to each other, and to share knowledge about spirits and cocktails.

In 2018 Bartender Atlas partnered with Gord Hannah and Jonathan Humphrey of The Drake Hotel to organize the now annual Toronto Cocktail Conference. TOCC is an education-focused conference that includes speakers from Toronto, across Canada and all over the world. The goal of TOCC is to continue building on an already strong community and to also introduce and educate new or less experienced bartenders to ideas, methods, history, and opinions of some of their more accomplished peers.

BUY THE TICKET, TAKE THE RIDE*

1 ½ oz (45 ml) Espadin mezcal (Los Siete Misterios Doba-Yej)
½ oz (15 ml) peach schnapps (Dillon's Small Batch Distillers)
1/3 oz (10 ml) Honey syrup (p. 197)
¾ oz (22.5 ml) lime juice
Mist of Bittered Sling Kensington Bitters
Sal de chapulin

Glass: Old-Fashioned / Rocks

Method: Rinse glass with bitters, rim the glass with sal de chapulin. Shake ingredients with ice and junk strain into glass.

EVELYN CHICK

Evelyn's career in hospitality started in Vancouver, and she quickly got recognition in the Canadian bartending scene for her unique approach to flavors. Throughout the years she has accumulated qualifications such as the BarSmarts certification, and Certified Specialist of Spirits, while finding success in multiple national and international cocktail competitions, including a win at the 2015 global Beefeater MIXLDN championships, representing Canada against 31 other countries. She was given the opportunity to travel the world promoting Canadian cocktail culture.

She now runs the bar program at one of the top bars in the country, PrettyUgly Bar in Toronto. Drawing from her experiences in leadership, she is an advocate for building a solid, inclusive, and integrated bar community within the Canadian market. A few years ago, she took over as the Canadian coordinator of Speed Rack, an all-female charity speed bartending competition. Alongside Christina Veira, they hope to build a platform in which female bartenders can showcase their skills in a male-dominated industry, while simultaneously raising funds for breast cancer research and education. She has taken on the project as co-curator of the Bar & Beverage Pavilion for Restaurants Canada Show 2019, building dynamic, forward-thinking educational programming for the restaurants industry. She is thrilled to be involved with our industry's rapid growth.

ENDLESS ENGLISH SUMMERS**

1 ¾ oz (52.5 ml) gin (Beefeater)
½ oz (15 ml) fino sherry
½ oz (15 ml) Green Park cordial (p. 196)
3 dashes Salted absinthe (p. 205)

Glass: Small Cocktail / Nick & Nora
Method: Stir all ingredients with ice and strain
Garnish: Pomelo twist

SANDY DE ALMEIDA

Sandy is a Toronto-based bartender and cocktail consultant. She launched Kindling in 2007, a pop-up that, according to the Globe and Mail, "helped school Toronto on how to make a proper drink and introduced sturdy cocktails to a city that was still under the influence of flavored-vodka Martinis." Six-time winner of *NOW* magazine's reader's poll's Best Bartender in Toronto award, she has judged several Toronto cocktail competitions, including Speed Rack Toronto, Bacardi Legacy, and Rematch Toronto. You can find her at The Drake Hotel.

RUST AND BONE**

2 oz (60 ml) Cedar-infused bourbon
(Four Roses) (p. 191)
½ oz (15 ml) Amaro Nonino
¼ oz (7.5 ml) Bénédictine
1 dash Angostura bitters

Glass: Old-Fashioned / Rocks
Method: Stir all ingredients with ice and
strained over large ice cube
Garnish: Cherry

ZAK DOY

Zak Barkley Doy has been in the spirits business for the past 18 years, evolving from the early days of slinging mocktails at Café Blue in Karachi, Pakistan, then flairing bottles in clubs and sports bars, and ultimately finding a love for cocktails that truly convinced him that this was his calling. In 2012, Zak won his first cocktail competition, beating some great bartenders and ultimately one of his very first mentors. It was a defining moment in setting out to become an architect of great cocktails and elixirs.

Currently, Zak continues to work as an independent consultant with his co-founded company, The Wizards of the West, spreading the love of fine spirits in Toronto and teaching a new generation of great bartenders. In addition, Zak continues building strong social media platforms to share his vision of cocktails and culture with his local and global community.

THE GREEN GODDESS*

2 oz (60 ml) gin (The Botanist)
1 oz (30 ml) fresh pressed ginger juice
1 oz (30 ml) lime juice
½ oz (15 ml) honey
5 slices of cucumber
8 leaves of mint

Glass: Old-Fashioned / Rocks
Method: Muddle all ingredients in shaker tin, add ice, shake and double strain.
Garnish: Celery curl and fresh cracked pepper

CHANTELLE GABINO

Chantelle is a born and raised Canadian bartender and industry professional with over a decade of experience in many facets of the hospitality industry. Growing up in beautiful British Columbia, her recent projects incorporate incentives to embrace sustainability, such as urban beekeeping and seasonality, in an effort to showcase mother nature's offerings. Utilizing her long-standing love of food and drink as well as her fine arts background she was named national winner of Bombay Sapphire's Most Imaginative Bartender competition in 2016 and was recently crowned the Bacardi Legacy 2018 national winner for Canada. Currently she is working as a Bittered Sling Ambassador, beverage director for the events company Mersey Cross, and bartender at The Drake Hotel in Toronto, all the while dedicating her free time to non-profit organizations. Chantelle is always ready and willing to shake things up.

CAMBIAR*

1 ½ oz (45 ml) aged rum (Bacardi Reserva Ocho)
½ oz (15 ml) amontillado sherry (Lustau Los Arcos)
½ oz (15 ml) Verjus
½ oz (15 ml) Simple syrup (p. 209)
1 dash Bittered Sling Clingstone Peach Bitters

Glass: Small Cocktail / Nick & Nora
Method: Throw ingredients over ice between two tins and strain
Garnish: Lemon twist and discard

ROBIN GOODFELLOW

Robin Goodfellow is the founder of Little Bones Beverage company and is part owner of the nationally and internationally award-winning Bar Raval, PrettyUgly, and Harry's in Toronto, as well as having many new projects on the go. He started bartending in 2003 in Toronto and talks about the constant need to change and evolve. His passion belongs to training new bartenders, fine tuning his existing establishments, helping new proprietors develop their bar programs, and throwing unique and creative events that push the beverage industry to new territory. Currently he is working on his Forward Drinking podcast.

GOTHIC QUARTER**

2 oz (60 ml) Garden-grown herb gin (p. 195)
½ oz (15 ml) rich syrup
1 oz (30 ml) fresh lime juice
4 dashes Peychaud's bitters

Glass: Large Cocktail
Method: Shake all ingredients with ice and double strain
Garnish: Seasonal herb sprig

DAVID GREIG

Starting off in a pub in North London, David has been behind bars of wildly varying repute for 18 years. He moved to Canada around the time of the 2010 Winter Olympics and was fortunate enough to work alongside Shaun Layton for the opening of L'Abattoir. Moving to Toronto for a change of pace in 2012, a stint at Ursa was followed by a move to Cocktail Bar, where he worked with Jen Agg developing the program there, before eventually helping to oversee cocktails for the Black Hoof Group. In September, he opened his first restaurant, Le Swan, with Jen Agg, Jake Skakun, and James Santon.

ABSINTHE WHIP**

¾ oz (22.5 ml) absinthe (Dillon's)
¾ oz (22.5 ml) orange liqueur (Cointreau)
1 oz (30 ml) tangerine juice
1 oz (30 ml) coconut cream
2/3 oz (20 ml) Pistachio orgeat (p. 202)

Glass: Large Cocktail
Method: Shake all ingredients with ice and double strain
Garnish: Three pistachios

JASON GRIFFIN

Jason Griffin didn't enter the bartending world by way of passion, but rather to support himself through his fine arts degree in Montréal in the early 2000s. Having never intended to continue bartending, Jason found himself moving up the ladder into fine dining, eventually leading him to the head bartender role at Daniel Boulud's Maison Boulud in the Ritz-Carlton Hotel. Inspired by his heavily-skilled and passionate peers, Jason developed a newfound vested interest in gastronomy and hospitality. After working in various management and ownership roles in Montréal, Jason then took on the bar manager role at the newly opened and highly acclaimed Hotel William Gray.

In 2017, Jason returned to his hometown of Toronto to head up the bar program at Bacchanal Restaurant. His extensive knowledge of spirits, gastronomy, and hospitality has made Bacchanal a go-to for local gourmands. In competition, Jason has won the national title at 2016 Grey Goose Pour Masters, the 2018 Dillon's Cocktail Cup, and 2017 Beefeater MIXLDN where he proudly represented Canada on the global stage.

CLAIRE DE LUNE**

1 2/3 oz (50 ml) aquavit
1 oz (30 ml) manzanilla sherry
1/6 oz (5 ml) Heavy syrup
(p. 210)
1 dash Salted absinthe (p. 205)
Thyme tincture (p. 208)

Glass: Large Cocktail
Method: Stir all ingredients except thyme tincture with ice. Spritz tincture over inside and outside of a chilled cocktail glass. Strain and serve.
Garnish: Basil leaf clipped to the side of the glass

BRAD GUBBINS

Gubbins is the co-owner of Founder restaurant and cocktail bar in Toronto's West End. With over two decades of industry experience, he has been fortunate to learn, train, and work with absolutely amazing individuals in both Europe and North America. Starting off his career in London and Leeds, he moved back to Canada and for the past 15 years has called Toronto home. He has the worked as well as opened some of the best bars and restaurants in the city, including Toronto Temperance Society, Spirithouse, and Founder. He has also played a leading role in helping train and mentor many in the Toronto hospitality industry and has helped to transform Toronto into a world-class bar and cocktail city.

FOR KING & COUNTRY*

1 oz (30 ml) calvados (Boulard)
¾ oz (22.5 ml) Berto Vermouth
½ oz (15 ml) Luxardo Bitter Bianco
2 dashes Black Cloud Charred Cedar Bitters

Glass: Small Cocktail / Nick & Nora
Method: Stir all ingredients with ice and strain
Garnish: Lemon zest with thyme and a cheese puff

H

The enigmatic bartender with the one letter name is as mysterious and eccentric as the space he occupies in space and time. Sitting at his bar feels like you are in Wes Anderson movie with John Malkovich on acid.

FLIPPING WINTER*

2 oz (60 ml) dark rum
1 oz (30 ml) gingerbread syrup (Monin)
2 oz (60 ml) flat chocolate ale/stout
1 whole egg

Glass: Mug
Method: Shake all ingredients with ice and double strain
Garnish: Grated cinnamon and nutmeg

NICK INCRETOLLI

Nick was born and raised in Hamilton, Ontario and has pursued his passion of working behind a bar since he was 18, giving him over 15 years of experience. He solidified his love for creating cocktails in 2013 when he entered his first local cocktail competition, and since then Nick has participated in numerous regional and national competitions—his proudest moment was winning a spot in 2017 Auchentoshan's New Malt Order and travelling to Scotland to create a whisky with other bartenders from around the world. Nick enjoys using spirits and ingredients in his cocktails in ways that challenge the norms. When Nick isn't behind the bar, he enjoys travelling to find new varieties of amaro to add to his home collection.

YOU DON'T MAKE FRIENDS WITH SALAD**

2 oz (60 ml) Campari
½ oz (15 ml) lemon juice
½ oz (15 ml) fresh grapefruit juice
1 oz (30 ml) Salted passion fruit syrup (p. 205)
Mushroom and black pepper foam (p. 201)
Handful of arugula

Glass: Large Cocktail
Method: Heavily muddle the arugula in a cocktail shaker, add all ingredients, shake with ice and double strain.
Top with prepared foam
Garnish: Freshly cracked black pepper on top of the foam

ROBIN KAUFMAN

Robin did a brief nine-month stint in the kitchen before moving behind the bar at Relish Gastropub. He then went on to UVA Wine Bar to broaden his newfound passion and hone his cocktail skills. He learned a lot at UVA and eventually became head bartender before moving to the Toronto Temperance Society where he spent five years or so as head bartender with Oliver Stern. Moving into high-volume bar Byblos allowed him to streamline the cocktail menu and be creative in a new environment. Finally, he accepted the bar manager job at Alo which evolved into a bar director role for the Alo Food Group, a company that includes Alo, Aloette, and Alo Bar Yorkville.

INFINITE JEST*

1 oz (30 ml) armagnac (Marie Duffau)
1 oz (30 ml) bianco vermouth (Iris)
1 oz (30 ml) amontillado sherry (Lustau)
½ oz (15 ml) apricot brandy (Giffard)
4 dashes Boker's Bitters

Glass: Large Cocktail
Method: Stir all ingredients with ice and strain
Garnish: Orange twist

NICK KENNEDY

Nick has been bartending for the last 12 years. Bartending is literally the only thing he has done with his professional life. He started tending bar in high school and university. During school, he worked at Salt Wine Bar for three years with his two best friends and future business partners, David Huynh and Cole Stanford. To his family's dismay, he dropped out of university to open Civil Liberties when he was 25, but they eventually came around. They built the bar on a shoestring budget, throwing themselves into the project for nine months straight and borrowing his mom's credit card to buy the back bar.

The first night was a huge success and after six months, they brought on Casey Ryan—a great friend and wonderful bar manager. As the venue progressed, partners came and went, a second venue called Vit Beo opened, great bartenders joined the team and he fell in love. Recently, they organised Miracle on Queen Street, a pop-up cocktail bar that raised $30,000 for a women's shelter. Currently, Nick is working on a new venue which is due to open in late 2019.

(PHO) KING DELICIOUS COCKTAIL***

2 oz (60 ml) Pho fat-washed vodka (p. 202)
¾ oz (22.5 ml) Lime cordial (p. 199)
Pinch of salt

Glass: Large Cocktail
Method: Shake all ingredients with ice and double strain
Garnish: Dehydrated lime wheel

CHRISTOPHER MCCRABB

Born and raised in the town of Meaford, Ontario, situated along the Georgian Bay, and with with both parents in the food and service industry, Christopher began his career in hospitality at a young age. However, it was while studying at the University of Toronto that he fell in love with the world of hospitality through the simplest interactions between guest and host. Christopher draws much of his inspiration from the mosaic of cultures that fill the city of Toronto. Although his approach to creating a cocktail experience may be described as playful, clean flavors resonate through his use of childhood memories of the four seasons along the Georgian Bay.

KEEPSAKE**

1 ½ oz (45 ml) gin (The Botanist)
½ oz (15 ml) fino sherry
¾ oz (22.5 ml) Evergreen tea syrup (p. 195)
¾ oz (22.5 ml) Citric acid solution (p. 193)

Glass: Small Cocktail / Nick & Nora
Method: Stir all ingredients with ice and strain
Garnish: Lemon twist

JESS MILI

What started as a part-time gig to pay her way through school has blossomed into a lifelong, passionate career for Jess. Her diligence and mastery of the craft have earned her a spot as one of Canada's top cocktail bartenders. Jess has a number of impressive competition wins under her belt, including the 2017 Bols Around the World global championship title and the 2018 Miss Speed Rack Canada title. Jess has spent the last couple of years travelling all over the world in pursuit of spirits and cocktail knowledge, most notably living in Oaxaca, Mexico to immerse herself in mezcal. You can find Jess wearing a smile behind the bar at Civil Liberties in Toronto, where she has been crafting fine cocktails since 2016.

SMALL TALK**

1 ½ oz (45 ml) Strawberry-infused gin (Beefeater) (p. 000)
½ oz (15 ml) Bols Genever
½ oz (15 ml) Green Chartreuse
1/3 oz (10 ml) Cynar
5 drops Saline solution 10% (p. 205)

Glass: Small Cocktail / Nick & Nora
Method: Stir all ingredients with ice and strain
Garnish: Grapefruit twist

LEAH MUCCIARONE

Leah grew up in a small town in wine county Niagara with a mother, who was involved in the wine and cheese industry. She moved to Toronto to study sign language interpretation and while in school was quickly drawn to the bustling energy of the Toronto restaurant industry. She started bartending the day she turned 19 and hasn't looked back. She has worked from the chaotic nightclubs of King St. to fine dining restaurants, and has spent the last five years working at Bar Isabel, bartending and tending to the rooftop garden. Her curiosity in the production and origin of spirits has caused her to travel as often as possible. Over the past few years, she has travelled to Peru and Mexico, discovering how tradition and cultivation play a role in the production of pisco and mezcal. Currently she is working at Midfield Wine Bar and moonlighting at Civil Liberties when given the chance.

¡AY MUCCISMO!**

1 ½ oz (45 ml) blanco tequila (Olmeca Altos)
½ oz (15 ml) Coffee Ancho Chili Campari
¼ oz (7.5 ml) dry vermouth (Dolin Dry)
¼ oz (7.5 ml) Cocchi Americano
5 drops Bittermens Xocolatl Mole Bitters

Glass: Old-Fashioned / Rocks
Method: Stir all ingredients with ice and strain over a 2" ice cube
Garnish: Grapefruit twist

ALANA NOGUEDA

Joining the Toronto hospitality community in 2009 by way of Las Vegas, Alana left her mark on a variety of cocktail bars in the downtown area, including the now-closed institution Harbors Room, before opening and helming The Shameful Tiki Room since 2015.

NO WOMAN, NO CRIME*

1 ½ oz (45 ml) amber rum (Smith & Cross)
½ oz (15 ml) Cynar
½ oz (15 ml) Honey syrup (p. 197)
¼ oz (7.5 ml) Ancho Reyes

Glass: Small Cocktail / Nick & Nora
Method: Stir all ingredients with ice and strain
Garnish: Grapefruit twist and discard

AVIVA ROSNICK

Aviva came to the cocktail bartending world by way of rock 'n' roll dive bars. She currently calls The Gift Shop Cocktail Bar in Toronto her home and draws upon music, pop culture, and film as inspiration for creating drinks.

HEATHEN CHILD*

1 oz (30 ml) blended Scotch (Ballantine's)
¾ oz (22.5 ml) dry vermouth (Noilly Prat)
½ oz (15 ml) Strega
½ oz (15 ml) madeira
1 Drop of 'Bar40' Umami Bitters

Glass: Small Cocktail / Nick & Nora
Method: Stir all ingredients with ice and strain
Garnish: Lemon twist and discard

JUSTIN SHIELS

Justin is a proclaimed connoisseur of the food, drink and hospitality industry, and actively seeks to improve his existing knowledge and skills, before using those experiences to empower others who have the desire and passion to thrive within the same industry.

He started in hospitality 14 years ago as a chef, developing and honing his craft for the following seven years, working in some of the top Canadian restaurants including Susur Lee, Splendido, Au Pied Du Cochon, and Toque, before settling into and applying these skills behind the bar for the past seven years.

FINO COLADA***

12.5 oz (375 ml) aged rum (Bacardi Ocho)
8.5 oz (250 ml) fino sherry
27 oz (800 ml) Pineapple coconut cordial (p. 202)
5 oz (150 ml) lime juice
5 oz (150 ml) 3.5% homogenized milk
Top with crémant or dry sparkling white wine

Batch Method: Combine all ingredients with the exception of the milk and sparkling wine. Chill in refrigerator for 48 hours to infuse all ingredients together. Bring milk to a simmer and add slowly to cold punch with an additional 2 oz (60 ml) of lime juice. Let curdle and rest for 30 seconds to allow milk proteins to bind with other fats and "impurities" in the punch. Using a Superbag (or alternatively you can line a colander or large strainer with linen cloth) with a large Cambro underneath and slowly pour the clotted punch, being sure to fill the strainer so as to coat it with milk solids. Allow to pour through for 1 minute or so, and then pour back the initial filtered punch to start the complete clarification filtration.

Glass: Small Cocktail / Nick & Nora
Serving Method: Pour 3.5 oz (105 ml) of punch and top with crémant or dry sparkling white wine
Garnish: Dehydrated lime wheel and parasol

IN FOCUS

KELSEY RAMAGE
& IAIN GRIFFITHS
TRASH TIKI

Trash Tiki is the anti-waste punk pop brainchild of bartenders Kelsey Ramage and Iain Griffiths. Launched at the end of 2016, Trash Tiki has become the bartender's resource for all things environmentally minded. Originally planned to be nothing more than an online platform to share recipes, the response quickly led the pair to start doing a series of pop-ups.

By early 2017, Trash Tiki took off, literally, with Kelsey and Iain leaving London and their positions at the world-renowned Dandelyan to embark on a 10-month world tour with the aim of bringing their anti-waste drinks message and transparent attitude to every corner of the globe.

With a strapline like "Drink Like You Give a Fuck", it was pretty clear what Trash Tiki's mission was from the get-go: To inject some fun, honesty, and creativity into the dull notion of sustainability. With the punk attitude well and truly alive in both of them, it then became about creating recipes that were open source for all to copy, enjoy, and improve.

The reception since first launching has now taken the pair to over 100 markets globally, with an estimated 3,000-plus bartenders having already received their environmentally minded education, firmly cementing the idea of sustainability as part of a modern bartender's skillset.

With anti-waste practicalities now firmly in the mind of bartenders around the globe, the high-energy chaos of those first pop-ups has manifested itself into more brands and platforms. Wasteland Paradise is the late-night, safe-space disco party the duo felt was missing from the many cocktail weeks and conferences held around the world. Common Sense, Kelsey's own platform to bring modern cocktails and environmental practises to the everyday drinker with a lifestyle and travel perspective, has launched to great response.

With all these now nestled under The Trash Collective company, Kelsey and Iain call Toronto home, and have much more planned in the years to follow. Trash Tiki has become a common name in the bartending world. Bigger than its two creators, it forms part of the global conversation the food and drink world is in the middle of—one in which everyone on either side of the bar is a participant.

To have a greater respect for the products used and consumed, to end the twentieth-century attitude of single-use ingredients, and to do all that with a light-hearted, fun, and hospitable attitude—that is what Trash Tiki stands for every time they scream "drink like you give a fuck".

POIRE-ING BLOOD** BY IAIN GRIFFITHS

1 1/3 oz (40 ml) gin (Ford's)
½ oz (15 ml) Poire Williams
½ oz (15 ml) Watermelon rind cordial (p. 209)
1/3 oz (10 ml) Lemon stuice
(p. 199)

Glass: Large Cocktail
Method: Shake all ingredients
with ice
Garnish: Few drops of
Peychaud's bitters

BLUSHING MAGGIE**
BY KELSEY RAMAGE

1 oz (30 ml) blanco tequila
(Tequila Cabeza)
½ oz (15 ml) bianco vermouth
(Dolin)
1/3 oz (10 ml) Chopping
board cordial (p. 192)
scant ½ oz (12.5 ml) Lemon stuice (p. 199)
1 barspoon Aperol
2 dashes orange bitters

Glass: Large Cocktail
Method: Shake all ingredients with ice and double strain
Garnish: Lemon dime discard

OWEN WALKER

Owen has been bartending for 12 years now and is responsible for El Rey Mezcal Bar, Quetzal, and the beverage programs of Rosalinda. He is soon to take over at Libretto Pizzeria. He is a passionate champion of agave spirits, sherry, and anything pineapple. Additionally, Owen is a partner in Capo Capo Aperitivo and Parasol Wine and Spirits.

PINEAPPLE DAIQUIRI*

1 ¾ oz (52.5 ml) white rum (Havana 3 year)
¾ oz (22.5 ml) Plantation Pineapple Rum
¾ oz (22.5 ml) Pineapple gomme syrup (p. 202)
1 oz (30 ml) lime

Glass: Large Cocktail
Method: Shake all ingredients with ice and double strain
Garnish: Cucumber slice and sal gusano

MICHAEL WEBSTER

A born and bred Torontonian, Michael is a cocktail consultant and former owner of some of Canada's best restaurants and bars including Bar Raval, PrettyUgly Bar, and Harry's. He has been in the industry for over 20 years and is a self-proclaimed Trader Vic disciple. He is currently building a non-alcoholic beverage brand, writing a book, developing a bar/cocktail/old-timey podcast while freestyle rapping on the Sidecar.

A WOMAN SCORNED**

1 ¾ oz (52.5 ml) bourbon (Buffalo Trace)
½ oz (15 ml) Averna Amaro
1/3 oz (10 ml) Campari
¼ oz (7.5 ml) Deathwish cane syrup (p. 194)
5 drops Cinnamon-clove tincture (p. 192)
5 dashes Bittermens Xocolatl Mole

Glass: Old-Fashioned / Rocks
Method: Stir with ice and strain over inch by inch ice cubes
Garnish: Grapefruit twist, express and discard

JULIANA 'ANA' WOLKOWSKI

Ana's first memory is cracking the tops off Molson Export, age four, behind her father's bar. When your earliest experience is keeping the population of St. Catharine's well oiled, there is a certain inevitability to a career that has led to her heading up the team at one of Canada's most respected and well-known cocktail bars. A leading authority on sherry, she has also competed in and won national competitions on several occasions. From late-night snack bars to dive bars, she has the well-rounded resumé of a seasoned professional, but has specialized in making some of the best cocktails in Toronto for five Canadian years as the bar manager at Bar Raval, the all-day-and-night temple to Spanish food and drink.

TEN LAST YEARS*

2 oz (60 ml) Canadian whiskey (Lot 40)
½ oz (15 ml) Barbadillo oloroso sherry
¼ oz (7.5 ml) Bénédictine
¼ oz (7.5 ml) Amaro Sibilia

Glass: Small Cocktail / Nick & Nora
Method: Stir all ingredients with ice and strain
Garnish: None

NOVA SCOTIA

ONE OF CANADA'S smallest islands is also one of the most densely populated, situated in the far east of the country. Nova Scotia is one of the islands that make up the Maritimes. The Scottish-influenced architecture in Halifax dots along the water, while the rest of the countryside feels like you've stumbled upon hidden glens in the hillsides of the UK. Authentic service is paired with incredibly knowledgeable bartenders and hospitality professionals to create an amazing culture that inspires much larger cities.

HALIFAX

I FIRST VISITED Halifax years ago, initially for a short-lived bar show and secondly for a private event around Christmas. The city immediately reminded me of Victoria and, in turn, felt homely and recognisable. Directly on the water, old buildings intermingle with new, and the Maritime hospitality shines through at every venue. I met Cooper Tardival before he moved to Vancouver and became one of the breakout talents on the west coast. On my second visit, I had the pleasure to meet cocktail culture pioneer and Diageo World Class Canada winner Jenner Cormier at Noble, the speakeasy under Middle Spoon. As I walked through the heavy door into the dark space, I knew that Halifax had a light burning that was ready to explode.

Fast forward to now and Jenner and Cooper, along with a swath of amazing bartenders, have created a world-class city with amazing food and drink. Bartenders like Shane Beehan, Will Irvine, and Jeff Van Horne regularly make it to World Class and Bacardi Legacy, taking with them the aspirations of the town's younger bartenders. Halifax, like many cities in Canada, has grown into a destination for food and drink. From fine-dining restaurants to local spirits, Halifax has the east coast covered.

SHANE BEEHAN

Shane Beehan is an east coast bartender, born in Newfoundland and raised in Nova Scotia. He currently calls Halifax his home, sharing it with his wife, daughter, and dog. With a decade of experience in the hospitality industry he has won many local and national awards. He is the 2016 Disaronno Canada Mixing Star winner, three times Diageo World Class national finalist, and two times Bacardi Legacy national finalist. In his hometown of Halifax, he has been awarded best bartender four years running. He has been published in various national and international publications, including the Field Guide to Canadian Cocktails. In his spare time, he likes to swim in the ocean and hike through the deep woods.

GIN AND SPRUCE**

1 ½ oz (45 ml) gin
(Compass Distilling Wild Gin)
½ oz (15 ml) aquavit
(Compass Distilling Aquavit)
¾ oz (22.5 ml) lemon juice
½ oz (15 ml) spruce-lemon oleo saccharum
¼ oz (7.5 ml) orgeat

Glass: Large Cocktail
Method: Shake all ingredients with ice and double strain
Garnish: Lemon twist and spruce tip

MATT BOYLE

Matt was born and raised in Dartmouth, Nova Scotia. He started in the hospitality industry at 16, and, working at various resorts and hotels in Nova Scotia, Matt got immersed in the world of client service. In his mid-twenties, he got his craft cocktail start at the Bicycle Thief Restaurant in Halifax, under the tutelage of Jeffrey Van Horne, a long-time friend and mentor. Matt's work ethic and inter-personal skills led the way for him to be a natural at tending the bar. He quickly fell in love with craft and the community he found himself a part of. After years of crafting cocktails and managing bars from Halifax to Ottawa, Matt, along with Jeffrey Van Horne, co-founded The Clever Barkeep, Atlantic Canada's premiere cocktail catering and bar consulting service. Armed with a business management degree from Dalhousie University, he is no stranger to the business world and operating a private company.

An accomplished competition-circuit bartender, this 2016 Canadian winner of Bacardi Legacy has gained a reputation as a polished performer, a hard-working entrepreneur, and skilled bartender. His cocktail, The Ocho Watchman, placed in the top 16 at the 2016 Global Finals of Bacardi Legacy. Along with owning the Clever Barkeep, Matt is currently the portfolio ambassador for Bacardi in Atlantic Canada.

THE OCHO WATCHMAN*

1 2/3 oz (50 ml) aged rum (Bacardi Reserva 8 Años)
2/3 oz (20 ml) bianco vermouth (Martini)
½ oz (15 ml) Cynar
2 dashes Scrappy's Grapefruit Bitters
1 dash Angostura bitters

Glass: Small Cocktail / Nick & Nora
Method: Stir all ingredients with ice and strain
Garnish: Grapefruit twist

JEFF VAN HORNE

Jeffrey Van Horne is credited as one of the founding bartenders of the current cocktail renaissance in Halifax. As one of the first bartenders in the city to develop large-scale cocktail programs, Jeffrey has helped revolutionize the city's taste buds. Over the past 10 years he has developed, consulted, and created the bar programs at restaurants and bars such as The Bicycle Thief, Lot Six, Field Guide, The Carleton, The Canteen, and Studio East.

In 2016, Jeffrey, with a strong desire to share his passion and knowledge of the food and beverage industry, teamed up with good friend and great bartender Matt Boyle to launch their bartending catering company, The Clever Barkeep. Its mission is to revolutionize the drinking culture in Atlantic Canada by bring craft cocktails to large events, working with various liquor brands to help educate both industry professionals, students and consumers. Jeffrey and Matt have also created the Drink Atlantic cocktail festival under The Clever Barkeep brand.

OLD FORT*

1 ½ oz (45 ml) rum (Fortress Rum)
1 ½ oz (45 ml) Lillet Blanc
¼ oz (7.5 ml) elderflower liqueur (St. Germain)
2 dashes Compass Distillers Grapefruit Bitters

Glass: Old-Fashioned / Rocks
Method: Stir all ingredients with ice and strain over large ice cubes
Garnish: Flamed orange zest

WILL IRVINE

Williston Irvine is a Halifax born and raised bartender who started off in the service industry as a barista in high school. Following a quick stint as a bread baker, he fell in love with making cocktails. Bartending for just three years, he now works at Bar Kismet and loves what he does and the team with whom he works. Will quickly became a bourbon fiend with a strong love for fortified wines and amari. A multiple national cocktail competition finalist, he is the next generation of Halifax bartenders.

JUKEBOX GRADUATE*

1 ¼ oz (52.5 ml) Cocchi Americano
1 oz (30 ml) manzanilla sherry
¾ oz (22.5 ml) bourbon (Wild Turkey Rare Breed)
3 dashes Angostura bitters

Glass: Small Cocktail / Nick & Nora
Method: Stir all ingredients with ice and strain
Garnish: Grapefruit twist

LINDSAY JONES

Originally from Toronto, Lindsay moved to Halifax three years ago where she began working for The Middle Spoon and its speakeasy bar Noble. She loves competing and has been lucky enough to be a part of numerous competitions on local, regional, and national levels. She is very passionate about her craft and has become an advocate for growing and showcasing all the amazing talent on the east coast.

ROSE COLOURED GLASSES*

1 ½ oz (45 ml) reposado tequila (Cazadores)
½ oz (15 ml) cognac (Courvoisier VS)
½ oz (15 ml) Dubonnet
2 dashes Bittered Sling Malagasy Chocolate Bitters
1 barspoon agave syrup

Glass: Small Cocktail / Nick & Nora
Method: Stir all ingredients with ice and strain
Garnish: Lemon twist

ANDREW KEYES

Keyes started his career in the hospitality industry growing up in his grandparents' butcher shop in Brantford, Ontario, cutting off pigs ears at the age of eight. He began working in restaurants at 15 years old as a line cook and eventually went to culinary school in Ottawa. After graduating he went to work in the East Village in New York City. Following five years in the kitchen, he took a break from the industry and went to business school in Ottawa. During that time, he was bussing tables and met his first mentor, Matt Boyle, from whom he learned how to bartend. This spark led him to fall in love with the craft and drop out of school. He now bartends at Lot Six.

QUEST OF THE PARSNIP**

1 ½ oz (45 ml) blanco tequila (Don Julio)
1 oz (30 ml) lemon juice
¾ oz (22.5 ml) parsnip juice
½ oz (15 ml) Simple syrup (p. 209)
4 dashes Peychaud's bitters

Glass: Large Cocktail
Method: Shake all ingredients with ice and double strain
Garnish: Sage leaf

KEEGAN MCGREGOR

In 2009, when he turned 19, Keegan started slinging beers at music venues in Moncton, New Brunswick, with no real knowledge of how to build a proper cocktail. After a few years, he decided to follow his musical passion and moved to St. John's, Newfoundland, where he began playing mandolin and bass in bands, and bartending on the side to help pay for life on the road. He eventually landed the head bartender position at The Adelaide Oyster House, which promptly kicked off his career as a cocktail bartender. Eventually his passion for music became more of a hobby, and his hobby as a bartender became more of a career. He moved to Halifax in 2017 to follow his new career focus and in 2018 was offered the head bartender position at Field Guide, where you can find him shaking up Daiquiris.

NONINO FRESCO*

1 ½ oz (45 ml) Amaro Nonino
½ oz (15 ml) curaçao (Pierre Ferrand)
1 oz (30 ml) grapefruit juice
¾ oz (22.5 ml) lime juice
¼ oz (7.5 ml) Simple syrup (p.209)
2 dashes orange bitters
3-5 mint leaves
splash of soda water

Glass: Highball / Collins
Method: Shake all ingredients except soda with ice, add soda and strain over ice.
Garnish: Grapefruit slice and mint sprig

PREP RECIPES

Preparation or "Prep Recipes" as we call them is all the mise-en-place we create before the doors of the bar open. As with wrangling over 150 bartenders from across the country, I tried to standardize recipes as close as I could.

ACIDIFIED GRAPEFRUIT JUICE

500g grapefruit juice
50g citric acid
Method: Combine both ingredients. Shake to combine. Bottle and refrigerate.

ACIDIFIED TOMATILLO JUICE

13 2/3 oz (400 ml) fresh tomatillo juice
94g filtered water
4g citric acid
2g malic acid
Method: Mix all ingredients together until acids dissolve. Bottle and refrigerate.

BLACK PEPPER SYRUP

1 cup black peppercorns
2 cups granulated sugar
2 cups water
Method: Crack peppercorns with a mortar and pestle. Gently heat the cracked peppercorns in a pot to aromatize. Add water and sugar and bring to a boil to dissolve sugar. Remove from heat and let cool. Fine strain and bottle.

BROWN BUTTER-WASHED COLD-BREW COFFEE AND HONEY SYRUP

500g honey
100g hot water
75g course coffee grounds
120g butter
Method: Dissolve honey and hot water. Add coffee to honey syrup and let steep for a week. Fine strain. Brown butter in a saucepan and add to coffee and honey syrup. Stir thoroughly and place in refrigerator overnight. Crack the butter on top and strain through cheese cloth multiple times until clear.

CANDY CAP-INFUSED RYE

20g dehydrated candy cap mushrooms
16 2/3 oz (500 ml) Lot 40 Rye

Method: Combine and let stand for 24 hours. Strain and bottle.

CEDAR BOURBON

50g cedar chips
25 oz (750 ml) bourbon (Four Roses)
Method: Place ingredients into a Mason Jar. Agitate. Let stand for 4 hours. Fine strain and bottle.

CEDAR RYE

4-inch section of a cedar shim
40 oz (1140 ml) Wiser's Deluxe
Method: Sterilize the cedar shim by first scrubbing off any dirt or dust and then soaking in warm saltwater for 1 hour. Soak in fresh water to remove any saltiness left in the wood. Chop the wood down and put in a clean glass jar with the Wiser's. Let stand for 6 days and then filter out all wood particles from the rye using a paper filter.

CHAMOMILE SYRUP

2 chamomile tea bags
300g hot water
300g sugar
Method: Steep chamomile tea bags in hot water for 5-10 minutes. Remove tea bags and add sugar. Stir until dissolved. Bottle and refrigerate.

CHAMOMILE TINCTURE

100g chamomile flowers
1kg vodka
Method: Combine in Mason Jar and infuse for 4 days. Fine strain. Bottle

CHAMOMILE & LAVENDER SYRUP

500g sugar
500g water
1 tbsp chamomile
2 tbsp lavender
Method: Combine sugar and water in a pot and bring to a simmer until sugar is dissolved. And chamomile and lavender and let steep for half an hour. Fine strain. Bottle and refrigerate

CHAMOMILE MAPLE SYRUP

1 tbsp chamomile tea
1 cup maple syrup
½ cup boiling water
Method: Warm over low heat for 10 minutes to infuse. Strain chamomile. Bottle and refrigerator.

CHAMPAGNE STRAWBERRY ACID

470g water
15g tartaric acid
15g lactic acid
500g Giffard strawberry syrup

Method: Mix in a Mason Jar. Shake to combine. Bottle and refrigerate.

CHARRED PINEAPPLE, ALLSPICE & CLOVE-INFUSED AÑEJO RUM

40 oz (1140 ml) Havana Club Añejo
1 pineapple sliced thin
5 allspice pods
5 cloves
Method: Char pineapple on grill. Combine with rum and spices in a clean container. Stand overnight. Fine strain and bottle.

CHERRY SHRUB

1lb Pitted Okanagan cherries
1 ½ cups white sugar
1 ½ cups apple cider vinegar
Peel of 1 lemon
Method: In a saucepan, start to macerate the cherries. Once the cherries have started to break down, add the sugar and apple cider vinegar. Bring to a simmer then add the peel of one full lemon and simmer for 20 minutes. Take off the heat and let cool. Fine strain. Bottle and refrigerate.

CHOPPING BOARD CORDIAL

1kg mixed fresh citrus off cuts
1kg water
240g granulated sugar
24g citric acid powder
12g malic acid powder
Method: Combine water and citrus off cuts. Let stand overnight at room temperature. Strain and add sugar and acids. Stir until dissolved. Fine strain. Bottle and refrigerate.

CINNAMON-CLOVE TINCTURE

20g cloves
20g Mexican cinnamon
¼ oz (7.5 ml) green Chartreuse
1 ¾ oz (52.5 ml) Everclear / over proof neutral grain spirit
2 oz (60 ml) spring water
Pinch of salt
Method: Place all ingredients in sterilized jar. Close and let stand for 3-5 days, shaking often. Add spring water and salt and shake well. Fine strain. Pour into 4 oz tincture bottle.

CINNAMON SYRUP

500g sugar
250g water
3 cinnamon stick
Method: Place all ingredients in a pot and bring to a boil. Take off heat and let stand for 15 minutes. Fine strain. Bottle and refrigerate.

CITRIC ACID SOLUTION

50g citric acid powder
250g warm water
Method: Combine in container.
Stir until dissolved. Cool and
bottle.

CITRIC WATER

20g citric acid powder
1kg hot water
Method: Combine and stir until
dissolved.

COCONUT SYRUP

500g sugar
500g coconut cream
Method: Combine all ingredients
in a pot and bring to a simmer
until sugar is dissolved. Bottle
and refrigerate.

COFFEE ANCHO CHILI CAMPARI

5g dried Arbol chilis
5g dried Ancho chilis
15g whole coffee beans (decaf
can also work)
25 oz (750 ml) Campari
Method: Combine all ingredients
and let sit for 4 hours. Fine strain.
Bottle.

COFFEE-INFUSED SWEET VERMOUTH

250g Bows & Arrows Coffee
Beans

33 ½ oz (1L) Cinzano Rosso
Method: Combine and infuse for
12 hours. Fine strain. Bottle and
refrigerate.

COFFEE BEAN-INFUSED CYNAR

16 2/3 oz (500 ml) Cynar
50g coffee beans
Method: Combine and let
macerate for 1 hour. Strain. Bottle
and refrigerate.

CLARIFIED PEAR & GREEN PEA SYRUP

350g pear
125g frozen green pea
1kg water
15g lemon juice
2.5 ml Pectinex Spinzall
1kg sugar
1g malic acid
Pinch of potassium sorbate
Method: Blend all ingredients.
Strain over 400-micron bag.
Add Spinzall to clarify. Add
sugar, malic acid, and potassium
sorbate. Bottle and refrigerate.

CRIMINI MUSHROOM HENNESSEY

25 oz (750 ml) Hennessy VS
5 Cremini mushrooms
Method: Slice and pan fry the
Cremini mushrooms slowly to
release the flavor. Let mushrooms

cool, add cognac. Let steep for an hour. Fine strain and bottle.

CROWBERRY TEA

200g hot water
4 Délice Boréal Crowberry tea bags
Method: Place tea bags in hot water. Let steep for 5-8 minutes.

CUCUMBER FENNEL CORDIAL

175g cucumber juice
75g fennel juice
60g lime juice
2.5g citric acid
7g lime zest
½ oz (12 ml) vodka
315g sugar
Method: Fine strain all ingredients except sugar and add to a blender. Blend liquid and slowly add sugar until fully incorporated. Bottle and refrigerate.

CUCUMBER ICE CUBES

225g English cucumber
Method: Juice the cucumber. Fine strain. Mix with equal parts water. Fill inch by inch silicone ice cube tray. Freeze.

DEATHWISH CANE SYRUP

2 ½L water
13g whole black peppercorns
3 large pinches sea salt (Newfoundland Salt Company)
6 Madagascar vanilla beans (insides)
13g allspice berries
6.66g cloves
3 star anise flowers
6.66g cascara (dried coffee cherries)
13g Mexican cinnamon
1666g azucar morena (cane sugar)
Method: Bring water, peppercorns and salt to a boil. Reduce to a simmer, add vanilla beans, allspice berries, cloves, star anise flowers, cascara and Mexican cinnamon. Let simmer for 15-30 minutes. Remove from heat and stir in cane sugar until completely dissolved. Fine strain and add ½ oz Green Chartreuse. Bottle and refrigerate.

DON'S MIX

500g white grapefruit juice
250g cinnamon syrup
Method: Blend syrup and juice together thoroughly. Bottle and refrigerate.

ESPRESSO SYRUP

¼ lb (125g) dark coffee grounds
12 oz (360 ml) water
12 oz (340g) sugar
Method: Bring all ingredients to
a boil. Simmer for 20 minutes.
Cool and bottle.

EVERGREEN TEA SYRUP

100g evergreen tea (dried spruce,
pine, and cedar tips)
16 2/3 oz (500 ml) boiling water
Equal parts sugar
Method: Combine tea and water
together and steep overnight.
Strain off and add equal weight of
sugar. Bring to a boil until sugar
is dissolved. Take off heat and let
cool. Bottle and refrigerate.

FIRENZE TINCTURE

6 2/3 oz (200 ml) Bombay
Sapphire (preferably USA 47%
abv)
1 tbsp crushes red chilies
1 oz sautéed dry cured spicy
Tuscan salami
Method: Seal all ingredients in
a vacubag and sous vide for 20
minutes at 65°C (150°F). Freeze
and fine strain fat and cooked
remains. Place in dropper bottle.

FROOT LOOP ORGEAT

1 cup Froot Loops
1 cup sugar
1 cup boiling water

½ cup slivered almonds
1 tsp orange blossom water
Method: Use food processor to
mix all dry ingredients into a
coarse powder. Add boiling water
and orange blossom water and
stir until well integrated. Allow to
sit overnight in refrigerator. Fine
strain. Bottle and refrigerate.

GALA APPLE SHRUB

3 medium Gala apples
1 cup apple cider vinegar
½ cup turbinado
Method: Grate apples with
peel on. Place in a nonreactive
container. Add apple cider
vinegar and turbinado sugar.
Place in refrigerator for 24 hours.
Fine strain. Bottle and refrigerate.

GARDEN-GROWN HERB GIN

25 oz (750 ml) gin
100g mixed seasonal herbs (e.g.
candy mint, anise, hyssop, lemon
verbena, shiso)
Method: Combine ingredients.
Let stand overnight. Fine strain.
Bottle.

GEISHA SYRUP

1 tbsp coriander seed
1 stalk crushed lemongrass
7 kaffir lime leaves
33 ½ oz (1L) Simple syrup
(p. 209)

3 thumb-size slices of ginger chopped

Method: Gently toast all dry ingredients. Add simple syrup and bring to a simmer. Add ginger, remove from heat and allow to cool. Fine strain and bottle.

GENTIAN & WORMWOOD TINCTURE

3 1/3 oz (100 ml) vodka
2 tsp dried gentian
2 tsp dried wormwood

Method: Combine ingredients in a Mason Jar and screw on the lid. Let stand for 2 weeks, shaking every few days. Fine strain and store.

GEWÜRZTRAMINER SYRUP

25 oz (750 ml) Gewürztraminer
750g white sugar

Method: Add ingredients into a pot and bring to a simmer till sugar is dissolved. Remove from heat and cool. Bottle and refrigerate.

GINGER & HONEY SHRUB

3 knobs ginger, rough skin removed and chopped
5 oz (150 ml) honey
10 oz (300 ml) hot water
4 cups (1L) white sugar
10 oz (300 ml) apple cider vinegar

Method: Place ginger, honey and hot water in a food processor. Blend into a paste, then pour into a pot on an induction burner. Add sugar and vinegar and simmer over medium-low for 15 minutes. Pour unstrained into bottle. Refrigerate.

GINGER SYRUP

2kg water
2kg sugar
5g rosemary
2g cloves
10g red peppercorns
Equal weight ginger juice

Method: Place water and sugar in a pot and bring to a simmer to dissolve. Take off heat. Add dry herbs and spices and let infuse for 10 minutes. Fine strain and weigh. Add equal weight of freshly juiced ginger juice. Stir to combine. Bottle and refrigerate.

GREEN PARK CORDIAL

1.25kg granulated white sugar
2 unwaxed lemons (peeled, cut into rounds, keep peels)
1/2 pomelo (peel and fruit, keep peels)
1 fennel bulb (julienned)
1 heaping teaspoon caraway

seeds
1 heaping teaspoon fennel seeds
62g citric acid
25 oz (750 ml) water
Method: Combine 1/2 bulb
fennel, and the caraway and
fennel seeds in a large pot, turn
on heat to medium and lightly
toast herbs. Add water and let
infuse on low for 10 mins, add
sugar and stir until dissolved.
Transfer to Cambro or glass
container. Peel lemons and cut
the peeled lemons into thin
rounds, add lemon and all the
remaining ingredients including
1/2 bulb fennel. Let sit for 48
hours. Take the lid off and take
out all peels and lemon wheels
with tongs. Transfer ingredients
into a blender and lightly blitz.
Fine strain out solids. Bottle and
refrigerate.

GREEN TEA & SERRANO CHILI AMARO

25 oz (750 ml) vodka
2 Serrano chilies
4 tsp dried green tea leaves
4 oz (120 ml) agave syrup, or to
taste
½ oz (15 ml) Gentian &
wormwood tincture (p. 196)
Method: Place chilies and vodka
in a Mason Jar and let stand for
about 5 hours. Double-strain
liquid into Mason Jar. Add green

tea to jar and let stand for 3 hours.
Fine strain and add agave syrup
and tincture.

GRENADINE (JEFFREY MORGENTHALER'S RECIPE)

2 cups POM pomegranate juice
2 cups sugar
2 oz (60 ml) pomegranate
molasses
1 tsp (5 ml) orange blossom water
Method: Place all ingredients in
a pot and bring to a low simmer
until dissolved. Stir in remaining
ingredients. Allow to cool. Bottle
and refrigerate.

GUAVA SYRUP

500g guava juice (Ceres)
500g sugar
Method: Combine ingredients
and stir until sugar dissolves.

HONEY SYRUP

500g honey
500g hot water
Method: Combine in container
and stir until dissolved. Bottle
and refrigerate.

HONEY CHAI SYRUP

½ cup local honey
½ cup boiling water
1 tbsp herbal chai tea (Silk Road)

Method: Pour all ingredients into container and stir until honey is dissolved. Let cool, strain, and bottle.

HONEY CINNAMON SYRUP

500g honey
500g water
4 cinnamon sticks

Method: Place all ingredients in a pot and bring to a low simmer. Let simmer for 30 minutes. Fine strain. Bottle and refrigerate.

HONEY GINGER SYRUP

1 cup white sugar
1 cup water
1 large ginger root peeled and roughly chopped

Method: Place the sugar and water in a pot and heat on a stove. Bring to a boil then reduce heat and simmer for 10 minutes. Take off heat and add ginger. Steep for 25-30 minutes. Fine strain. Bottle and refrigerate.

HOUSE-MADE DRAMBUIE

Monkey Shoulder Infusion:
3g fresh nutmeg
6g sarsaparilla
6g cherry bark
3g cinnamon bark
2.4g cloves
3g aniseed
3g fennel seed
6 cardamom pods cracked
25 oz (750 ml) Monkey Shoulder

Method: Mix all ingredients and let infuse for 48 hours. Strain and begin second infusion.

25 oz (750 ml) Monkey Shoulder infusion
25 oz (750 ml) local honey
187.5g apricot
56.25g ginger sliced
56.25g orange zest
3 pinches fresh lavender flowers

Method: Combine all ingredients. Gently heat to melt honey. Let infuse for 24 hours. Strain and bottle.

JALAPENO SYRUP

500g boiling water
3 jalapenos
500g sugar

Method: Slice jalapenos and place in boiling water. Let sit for 2-3 mins. Add sugar and stir until dissolved. Let stand overnight. Fine strain. Bottle and refrigerate.

LAPSANG SOUCHONG MAPLE SYRUP

1 tsp lapsang souchong
250g hot water
500g dark maple syrup

Method: Steep lapsang souchong in water for 5-8 minutes. Strain and add to maple syrup. Stir to dissolve. Bottle and refrigerate.

LAVENDER SYRUP

1 cup water
1 cup white sugar
2 tbsp fresh or dried lavender
blossoms
Method: Combine water and
lavender in a pot. Bring water and
lavender to a boil. Take off heat,
add sugar and stir until dissolved.
Let lavender steep for 45 minutes.
Fine strain. Bottle and refrigerate.

LAVENDER TINCTURE

1 tsp dried orange peel
½ tsp dried lemon peel
2-inch piece vanilla bean
2 tbsp dried lavender flowers
1 ½ cups Everclear
1 ½ cups filtered water
Method: Infuse all ingredients
except filtered water for 1-2 days.
Fine strain. Add filtered water.
Bottle in a spritzer.

LEMON STUICE

1 ½L water
1kg lemon husks
70g sugar
20g citric acid
10g malic acid
Method: Bring water to a boil.
Add lemon husks and boil for
5 minutes. Remove pot from
heat and strain and press husks
to extract all liquid. Place liquid

back on heat without lid, bring to
boil then simmer and reduce by
one third of original weight. Add
sugar and acids until dissolved.
Measure volume and add equal
parts fresh lemon juice. Fine
strain. Bottle and refrigerate.

LEMON THYME SYRUP

1kg water
1kg sugar
3g thyme
3g lemon peel
Method: Combine water and
sugar in a pot and bring to a
boil. Combine the thyme and
lemon peel in a large container
or bowl. While the syrup is hot,
pour it into the container over the
lemon and thyme and let infuse
overnight. Fine strain. Bottle and
refrigerate.

LIME CORDIAL (NICK KENNEDY)

360g water
11g citric acid
7g malic acid
Zest of 20 limes
12 oz (360 ml) lime oleo
saccharum (p. 200)
Method: Combine water and
acids together and dissolve.
Combine acids, zest and lime
oleo saccharum in a pot. Bring to
a light simmer for 10-15 minutes.
Fine strain. Bottle and refrigerate.

LIME CORDIAL (JONATHON COTE)

13 1/3 oz (400 ml) fresh lime juice
Peel of 3 limes
150g sugar
2 tsp citric acid
Method: Double boil all ingredients until sugar is dissolved. Fine strain. Bottle and refrigerate.

LIME OLEO SACCHARUM

100g lime zest
200g sugar
100g water
Method: Combine lime zest and sugar in a Ziplock or vacubag and let stand for 18 hours. Strain lime zest out of syrup. Add water and combine thoroughly. Bottle and refrigerate.

LONG PEPPER TINCTURE

15g long peppercorn
4 oz (120 ml) Ketel One (or any high-proof vodka)
Method: Grind long peppercorn. Combine with vodka for 7 days in an airtight container. Shake once a day. Fine strain. Place in dasher bottle.

MILK LIQUEUR

500g whole milk
500g sugar
500g vodka or grappa
½ orange cut into wedges
½ lemon cut into wedges
Method: Put all ingredients into a large container or Mason Jar and combine. Cover with cheese cloth and let it sit at room temperature for 10-14 days, stirring once daily. Fine strain 2-3 times until clear. Bottle and refrigerate.

MINT FOAM

6 oz (180 ml) Simps Mint Syrup
3 oz (90 ml) lime juice
2 oz (60 ml) egg white
Method: Fine strain lime juice. Combine all ingredients in iSi and charge with N2O. Shake and refrigerate.

MIREPOIX SOUP

33 ½ oz (1L) chicken Broth
½ cup water
3 onions
1 bunch of celery
4 carrots
Knob of ginger
3 cloves of garlic
2 bell pepper
Method: Cut up onions, celery, carrots, along with ginger, sweet bell pepper and garlic and add to a pot. Add chicken broth, and half a cup of water. Simmer for 3 hours. Place in Vitamix and blend for 10 minutes. Strain through cheese cloth and a fine mesh

strainer. Season with salt, pepper, and fresh lemon juice. Bottle and refrigerate.

MUSHROOM SYRUP

3 oz (85g) dried Porcini mushrooms
3 cups (720 ml) water
2 cups granulated sugar
Method: Bring dried mushrooms and water to a boil and then let cool to extract flavour. Strain out mushroom pieces and bring mushroom water to a boil to reduce by about one third of the volume. Let cool, and strain through a coffee filter. Measure remaining volume of mushroom water and add an equal amount of sugar to a clean pot. Bring to a quick boil to dissolve the sugar. Bottle.

MUSHROOM & BLACK PEPPER FOAM

5 egg whites
3 oz (90 ml) mushroom syrup
3 oz (90 ml) black pepper syrup
2 oz (60 ml) kabosu juice
Method: Place all ingredients in a 1/2 litre iSi whipper. Seal and shake to incorporate ingredients. Charge with one N20 cartridge and shake. Charge with a second cartridge and shake again. Refrigerate.

MUSHROOM & CORN SYRUP

250g Porcini mushrooms
250g corn kernels
200g sugar
Method: Combine all ingredients in vacubag and seal tight. Place in sous vide at 28°C (80°F) for 12 days. Fine strain. Bottle and refrigerate.

ORANGE-ALOE CORDIAL

1kg aloe vera juice
1kg sugar
Peel of 4 oranges
Method: Combine ingredients in a pot. Bring to a boil then simmer for 10 minutes. Remove from heat and add 75g citric acid. Stir until it dissolves. Bottle and refrigerate.

ORGEAT

2 cups blanched almonds
4 cups water
Equal parts sugar
½ tsp orange blossom water
1 oz (30 ml) cognac
Method: Soak almonds in 2 cups of water for 30 minutes. Drain and add to blender with 2 cups of water. Blitz on high until a fine paste is formed. Strain through cheese cloth until all liquid from almonds has been extracted. Add equal parts sugar to the yield of almond milk. Add orange

blossom water and cognac. Bottle and refrigerate.

PARMESAN TUILE

100g grated parmesan
Method: Spread grated parmesan on baking sheet in disc shape. Bake in oven for 6 minutes at 200°C (400°F).

PEACH HONEY GINGER SYRUP

3 peaches (skinned and pitted)
60-70g skinned diced ginger
6 tsp honey
500g water
500g sugar
Method: Place all ingredients in a pot and bring to simmer. Allow to simmer for 10-15 minutes, constantly stirring. Cool and strain. Bottle and refrigerate.

PEACH BLACK TEA OLEO SACCHARUM

1kg turbinado sugar
Peel of 10 lemons
1kg boiling water
50g peach black tea (Silk Road)
Method: Mix sugar and lemon peels, muddle and let stand for 30 minutes to infuse. Steep tea in hot water for 5-8 minutes. Combine sugar/lemon mix and steeped tea together. Stir until sugar dissolves. Fine strain. Bottle and refrigerate.

PHO FAT-WASHED VODKA

25 oz (750 ml) vodka
150g pho broth fat
Method: Blend fat and vodka together in food processor. Place in freezer for 24 hours. Fine strain and bottle. Refrigerate.

PINEAPPLE COCONUT CORDIAL

125g coconut cream
125g sugar
18 oz (550 ml) pineapple juice
Method: Place all ingredients in a saucepan and bring to a low heat. Bottle.

PINEAPPLE GOMME SYRUP

500g fresh pineapple juice
500g sugar
30g gomme Arabic
3g citric acid
Method: Combine all ingredients in pot and bring to a high simmer. Let cool. Bottle and refrigerate.

PISTACHIO ORGEAT

500g sugar
500g hot water
350g pistachios
Method: Place all ingredients in blender and purée until smooth. Fine strain. Bottle and refrigerate.

PISTACHIO & APRICOT ORGEAT

200g unsalted pistachios
100g apricots
23 ½ oz (700 ml) water
600g sugar
5 ml orange flower water
Method: Place pistachios, apricots and water in a bowl and let stand for 4 hours. Add ingredients to a pan with sugar and bring to a gentle simmer until all sugar is dissolved. Place all liquid and solids into a blender and blend until smooth. Fine strain. Allow to cool to room temperature and add orange flower water. Bottle and refrigerate.

PORTOBELLO ESSENCE

5 Portobello mushrooms
Method: Thoroughly blend mushrooms. Pour mix into cheesecloth. Hard squeeze to extract liquid. Bottle and refrigerate.

QUEBEC HONEY SYRUP

250g Alvéole honey
250g water
Method: Place water in pot and bring to a simmer. Add honey and stir until dissolved. Bottle and refrigerate.

RABBIT CHASER SYRUP

1lb carrots
33 ½ oz (1L) water
8 1/3 oz (250 ml) grade-A maple syrup
Tablespoon of powdered cinnamon
Tablespoon of powdered cardamom
Tablespoon of caraway seeds
Pinch of salt
Method: Preheat oven to 165°C (325°F). Peel carrots. Take half and julienne for roasting. Liberally sprinkle cinnamon, cardamom, and caraway over carrots with oil and roast for 25-30 minutes. Take the other half of carrots and juice. In a saucepan add water, maple syrup, salt and roasted carrots. Let slowly reduce for 20 minutes on a mid to low temperature, do not boil. Fine strain. Let cool then add to fresh pressed juice. Bottle and refrigerate.

RICE ORGEAT

1kg rice
33 ½ oz (1L) water
Equal parts white sugar
Method: Preheat the oven to 160°C (315°F). On a baking tray, bake 500g of rice for 20 minutes. Place cooked rice in container and add 16 2/3 oz (500ml) water. Place 500g raw rice in container

and add 16 2/3 oz (500ml) water. Let both mixes infuse for 24 hours in the fridge. Strain and combine. Add equal weight of sugar to rice milks. Bring to boil until sugar is dissolved. Fine strain. Bottle and refrigerate.

ROASTED FENNEL SYRUP

1 bulb fennel
½ tsp salt
1 tsp oil
500g sugar
500g water
10 cracked fennel seeds

Method: Slice and roast bulb of fennel with the salt and olive oil until well browned. Place fennel, fennel seeds, sugar and water in a pot and reduce by half. Fine strain. Bottle and refrigerate.

ROAST PEACH SYRUP

4 peaches
500g water
500g sugar

Method: Cut peaches in half and pit. Place in a 9x13 baking dish and sprinkle lemon juice, sugar and maybe some herbs (basil or anise hyssop) on top. Bake in the oven at 190°C (375°F) for 12 minutes until caramelised. Combine sugar and water in a pot and simmer until dissolved. Remove peaches from oven.

Mash them thoroughly and add to sugar syrup and let steep in fridge for 2 days. Fine strain. Bottle and refrigerate.

ROOT BEER SYRUP (NATE CAUDLE)

50g sarsaparilla
50g sassafras
1kg water
1kg sugar

Method: Bring all ingredients to a high simmer until sugar dissolves. Simmer for 15 minutes. Fine strain. Bottle and refrigerate.

ROOT BEER SYRUP (GRANT SCENEY)

75g sassafras
8 cinnamon sticks
1 cup dried bay leaves
30 allspice berries
15 cloves
5 star anise
4 vanilla beans, sliced, opened, and scraped
2 tsp cinchona bark
3kg brown sugar
67 oz (2L) maple syrup
167 ½ oz (5L) water

Method: Bring all ingredients to a simmer for 10-15 minutes. Fine strain. Bottle and refrigerate.

ROOTS & BLUES SYRUP

Zest of 1 orange
Zest of 1 lemon

2 tsp sassafras
2 tsp sarsaparilla
2 tsp licorice root
2 tsp cassia chips
1 tsp hyssop
1 tsp wintergreen
1 tsp spearmint
5 star anise pods
5 green cardamom pods
1 cinnamon stick
750g water
750g brown sugar
Method: Bring all ingredients to a boil. Pour into Mason Jar, seal and shake. Let cool, shaking every 4 hours. Let stand for 24 hours. Strain, bottle, and refrigerate.

ROSEMARY SYRUP

1 cup white sugar
1 cup water
¼ cup rosemary leaves
Method: Place sugar and water in pot and bring to a boil. Add rosemary leaves and take off the heat. Let stand for 20-30 minutes. Fine strain. Bottle and refrigerate.

SAGE-INFUSED EMPRESS 1908 GIN

100g fresh sage
25 oz (750 ml) Empress 1908 Gin
Method: Combine ingredients and let stand overnight. Fine strain.

SAGE SYRUP

25g sage leaves
33 ½ oz (1L) Simple syrup (p. 209)
Method: Blanch sage leaves in boiling water for 30 seconds. Remove and rinse in an ice bath for 1 minute. Add sage leaves to blender with simple syrup and blend on high until thoroughly mixed. Fine strain. Bottle and refrigerate.

SALINE SOLUTION (10%)

250g hot water
25g kosher salt
Method: Combine and stir until dissolved. Bottle.

SALTED ABSINTHE

5g kosher salt
1 oz (30 ml) water
1 oz (30 ml) absinthe
Method: Dissolve salt into water. Mix salted water with absinthe. Bottle in dasher bottle.

SALTED PASSION FRUIT SYRUP

16 ¼ oz (480 ml) unsweetened passion fruit juice
2 cups granulated sugar
2 tsp kosher salt
Method: Bring all ingredients to a medium heat until sugar is dissolved. Bottle.

SARSAPARILLA-INFUSED FLOR DE CANA 4

25 oz (750 ml) Flor de Cana 4 year
30g sarsaparilla root
Method: Steep sarsaparilla root in rum for 12-24 hours. Fine strain. Bottle.

SERRANO-INFUSED MEZCAL

25 oz (750 ml) Los Siete Misterios Espadin
8g serrano pepper
Method: Add diced serrano peppers to mezcal. Infuse for 24 hours. Strain and bottle.

SMOKED ALDERWOOD TEA CORDIAL

2kg water
100g cedar chips
40g smoked alderwood tea
2kg sugar
90g citric acid
Method: Bring water to a boil. Add cedar and tea to water and steep for 20 minutes. Strain out solids. Add sugar and citric acid. Stir to dissolve. Bottle and refrigerate.

SMOKED CHERRY BITTERS

1 vanilla bean, split lengthways
¼ stalk lemongrass, cut into small pieces
1 star anise pod
1 juniper berry
1 clove
1 cardamom seed
¼ tsp anise seeds
¼ cup smoked dried cherries
1 cup rye whiskey
Method: Pit and halve cherries, hot smoke on BBQ with cherry wood for 15 minutes. Cool and place in dehydrator. Dehydrate for 24 hours or until moisture is removed. Combine all ingredients in an air-tight glass jar. Seal and shake. Let ingredients steep for 14 days, shaking once every other day. Fine strain and bottle.

SMOKED DRIED CHERRY SUGAR

250g cherries
250g sugar
Method: Pit and halve cherries, hot smoke on BBQ with Cherry wood for 15 mins, cool and place in dehydrator. Poweder using a mortar and pestle or food processor, add sugar until thoroughly mixed.

SMOKED PINEAPPLE

1 pineapple
Equal parts sugar
Method: Skin, core, and chop pineapple. Using a cold smoker and applewood chips, put

pineapple chunks in covered container and fill container with smoke. Smoke for 35-40 minutes. Juice the pineapple. Add equal parts sugar to pineapple juice. Put in pot on low heat until sugar is dissolved. Bottle and refrigerate.

SOUR CHERRY JAM

2 cups BC sour cherries, pitted and chopped
1 cup granulated sugar
1/2 tonka bean, grated
Cracked pepper to taste
Method: In a large deep skillet, add chopped cherries, sugar, and tonka bean. Heat and stir until it reaches a rolling boil. Boil and stir until it thickens after approximately 10 minutes. Remove from the heat and transfer to an 8-ounce jar. Let cool completely before using. Store in the refrigerator.

SPICED RAISIN CORDIAL

500g brown sugar
500g hot water
100g raisins
10 star anise pods
Method: Combine hot water, star anise pods and half of the raisins and allow to soak for 30 minutes. Take the remaining raisins and mix thoroughly into brown sugar. Combine both mixtures and stir until fully integrated. Fine strain. Bottle and refrigerate.

SPICED RIESLING SYRUP

20g fresh tarragon
15g fresh thyme
15g fresh parsley
15g fresh mint
25 oz (750 ml) dry German Riesling
750g sugar
Method: Let infuse for 48 hours. Fine strain. Combine with equal parts sugar and reduce by 20 percent over low heat. Bottle and refrigerate.

SPRUCE LEMON OLEO SACCHARUM

1 cup white sugar
Zest of 4 lemons
1 tbsp dried spruce powder
Method: Place all ingredients in vacuum bag. Vacuum seal package and let sit overnight until the oils have dissolved into the sugar. If sugar doesn't dissolve, sit in a bath of hot water. Fine strain. Bottle and refrigerate.

SPRUCE TIP TINCTURE

50g fresh spruce tips
250g neutral grain spirit with 50% abv
Method: Combine in a glass jar. Infuse for 7 days. Fine strain.

STRAWBERRY-INFUSED GIN

25 oz (750 ml) Beefeater Gin
Pint of strawberries
Method: Wash and slices strawberries. Place in Mason Jar and top with gin. Let stand for 3 days. Fine strain and bottle.

STRAWBERRY SYRUP

500g water
500g sugar
500g frozen strawberries
Method: Place all ingredients in a pot and bring to a boil, stirring occasionally. Turn down heat to low and simmer for 15 minutes. Take off heat and cool. Fine strain. Bottle and refrigerate.

TEPACHE

1 whole skinned and cored pineapple
1 habanero pepper
1 cup demerara sugar
8 cups water
Method: Place all ingredients in clean Cambro or container. Let sit at room temperature covered in cling wrap and allow the natural yeasts of the pineapple to ferment mixture for 3 days. Strain and bottle.

THYME HONEY SYRUP

500g honey
500g water
5 sprigs of thyme
Method: Bring honey and water to a low heat to dissolve. Add thyme and heat for 5 minutes. Remove from heat and let thyme steep for 15 minutes. Fine strain. Bottle and refrigerate.

THYME TINCTURE

1 oz (30 ml) vodka
1 large sprig of fresh thyme
Zest of 1 lemon
Pinch of salt
Method: Seal all ingredients in a vacuum bag or in a Mason Jar. Let stand for 1 week at room temperature. Strain and transfer to atomizer bottle.

TOMATILLO PULP & CILANTRO ROOT CORDIAL

100g tomatillo pulp
50g roughly chopped cilantro root
150g superfine white sugar
Method: Vacuum seal all ingredients together and let sit refrigerated for two days. Bring up to room temperature and pass through a fine strain. Bottle and refrigerate.

VANILLA-INFUSED RUM

25 oz (750 ml) Appleton 12 year
3 vanilla beans
Method: Split beans down
lengthways. Combine rum and
vanilla beans. Infuse for 24 hours.
Strain and bottle.

VANILLA SHRUB

16 2/3 oz (500 ml) apple cider
vinegar
8 1/3 oz (250 ml) water
250g sugar
3 vanilla beans
Method: Place all ingredients in
a pot and bring to a boil. Take off
heat and let stand for 24 hours in
the fridge. Fine strain. Bottle and
refrigerate.

VANILLA SYRUP

500g water
500g sugar
1 vanilla bean
Method: Split bean lengthways.
Place all ingredients in a pot and
bring to the boil. Take off heat.
Let stand for 15 minutes. Fine
strain. Bottle and refrigerate.

WATERMELON RIND CORDIAL

200g watermelon rinds, washed
400g sugar
Method: Cut watermelon rinds
into 2- to 4-inch pieces and put
in container. Add enough sugar
to cover, seal the container and
leave in a refrigerator for 12-24
hours. Stir remaining sugar into
mix. Place all ingredients in
blender and blend on high. Fine
strain. Bottle and refrigerate. Use
in 2-3 days.

WATERMELON SYRUP

500g watermelon flesh
500g white sugar
Method: Blend thoroughly until
sugar is dissolved. Fine strain
pulp out and bottle.

SWEETENING SYRUPS

"Oh, what fun we'll have" is the
exact way to talk about your house
sugar syrup. In my experience,
everyone has their house style or
styles of simple syrups. Here are the
few simple syrups, I have used over
the years.

SIMPLE SYRUP

500g white sugar
500g boiling water
Method: Mix and stir until
dissolved.

SOOLE'S HOUSE SYRUP

This is my weird house syrup
that I love. I have had many
conversations as to why I do this;

some maligned, some inquisitive.
After years behind the bar,
years of experimenting that the
1.5:1 turbinado to water is the
perfect ratio for brown and white
spirits, spirit forward to mixed.
Turbinado is a unique sugar in
that it's spun sugar cane juice
with molasses added. It needs
slow heat, never to be boiled;
boiling the dissolved sugars will
trigger the crystallization process
again. This, along with the longer
prep time, is the reason for it
being a bit harder but much more
rewarding.
750g turbinado syrup
500g water
Method: Bring sugar and water to
a low simmer until dissolved.

HEAVY SYRUP

1kg demerara sugar
500g water
Method: Bring sugar and water to
a low simmer until dissolved.

GLOSSARY

absinthe: A green liqueur flavoured with wormwood (or a substitute), anise, and other aromatics.

ABV: Stands for alcohol by volume. A standard measure of how much alcohol (ethanol) there is in an alcoholic beverage (expressed as a percentage of total volume). This standard is used worldwide.

acid phosphate: Gives a drink sourness without making it taste like anything in particular. Its inherent salts can enhance existing flavours, much as salt does with food.

Adonis: A fino sherry–based cocktail dating back to the late 1800s. Named after a Broadway play that ran for over 500 shows.

agave syrup: Made from the nectar of the agave plant, it can be used as an alternative sweetener in place of maple syrup, honey, or standard refined sugar.

Akvavit/aquavit: A strong, clear Scandinavian liquor distilled from potato or grain mash and flavoured with caraway seed and dill.

amaro: Italian for "bitter." An Italian herbal liqueur that is commonly consumed as an after-dinner digestif. It usually has a bittersweet flavour, is sometimes syrupy, and has an alcohol content between 16 and 35 percent.

amaretto: An Italian liqueur flavoured with almonds.

añejo rum: Aged rum. There are no legal definitions of what "aged" means; however, there are a few countries that have minimum aging requirements for rum production. For instance, Puerto Rico requires one year, and Venezuela requires two.

Angostura bitters: Aromatic bitters with flavours of gentian, clove, and allspice, most famously used in the Manhattan and the Old Fashioned.

Aperol: An Italian aperitif originally produced by the Barbieri Brothers company in Padua. Aperol is now produced by Gruppo Campari. Though it was created in 1919, Aperol did not become successful until after the Second World War. Its ingredients include, among others, bitter orange, gentian, rhubarb, and cinchona. It has an alcohol content of 11 percent.

aromatic bitters: Bitters that contain aromatic oils but few tannins.

atomizer: A device for emitting

212

water, perfume, or other liquids as a fine spray.

Bénédictine: A liqueur containing aromatic herbs and spices, originally made by Bénédictine monks in France.

blackstrap rum: Rum made with dark, viscous molasses, the by-product of the final extraction phase of sugar-refining.

blanco tequila: Blanco or silver tequila is tequila that has been aged no longer than six months in oak. Most producers distil, bring the alcohol content to the required amount, and bottle the tequila without it ever touching oak.

blended whisk(e)y: Whisky that is either a blend of two or more whiskies, especially a malt whisky and an unmalted grain whisky, or a blend of whisky and other neutral spirits.

Boulevardier: A cocktail that is part of the Negroni family. It uses the same ingredients but is fortified with bourbon instead of gin. First published in Harry McElhone's 1927 cocktail book *Barflies and Cocktails*.

bourbon whiskey: American whiskey that must consist of at least 51 percent corn, be aged in new charred-oak barrels at a minimum of 62.5 percent abv and be bottled at no less than 40 percent abv. Made predominantly in Kentucky.

Brooklyn: One of the New York borough cocktails, the most famous of which is, of course, the Manhattan. The Brooklyn is a twist on the basic DNA of the Manhattan. It uses rye, dry vermouth, maraschino liqueur, and one of the rarest liqueurs in the world, Amer Picon. Amer Picon is a French amer/amaro that has limited exportation throughout the world outside of France.

cachaça: Brazil's national spirit. Similar to rum but distilled from sugar cane juice rather than molasses.

Caipirinha: One of the best-selling drinks in Brazil. A mix of fresh, muddled lime, sugar (syrup or granulated), and cachaça.

calvados: A dry apple brandy made in Normandy, France.

Campari: An alcoholic aperitif made by infusing herbs and fruit (including chinotto and cascarilla) in alcohol and water. It is characterized by its dark red colour.

channelled twist: A thicker spiral of lemon zest cut with a channel knife.

Chartreuse: An aromatic green or yellow liqueur flavoured with orange peel, hyssop, and peppermint oils. Made at a monastery near Grenoble, France.

citric acid: A sharp-tasting crystalline acid, present in the juice of lemons and other sour fruits. It is a natural preservative and is used to add an acidic, or sour, taste to foods and drinks.

Cocktail à la Louisiane: In Stanley Clisby Arthur's

book *Famous New Orleans Drinks and How to Mix 'Em*, published in 1937, he explained that the Cocktail à la Louisiane was the house cocktail at the Restaurant de la Louisiane, "one of the famous French restaurants in New Orleans, long the rendezvous of those who appreciate the best in Creole cuisine." The cocktail uses rye, sweet vermouth, and Benedictine, with hints of absinthe or Herbsaint and dashes of Peychaud's bitters.

Collins: An iced drink made with gin (Tom Collins) or vodka, rum, whisk(e)y, etc., mixed with soda water, lime or lemon juice, and sugar. Also, a style of tall glass.

cordial: A strong, highly flavoured sweet liquor usually consumed after a meal.

crème de cacao: A sweet liqueur flavoured with vanilla and cacao beans.

crème de cassis: A sweet, dark red liqueur made from blackcurrants.

Crusta: By definition can have any spirit as its base. It is a particular small style of drink, which seems to require two things to make it legitimate: A frosted wine glass rimmed with sugar and the entire peel of a lemon or orange fitted into the glass.

Cynar: An Italian bitter liqueur made from 13 herbs and plants, predominantly the artichoke (Cynara scolymus), from which the drink derives its name.

dark rum: Aged longer than clear white rum, usually in heavily charred oak barrels. It also possesses a far greater flavour than white rum or even gold rum, usually with a sweeter taste.

drinking vinegar: Certain vinegars (apple cider, for example) can be used as a daily tonic to change the body's pH from acidic to alkaline.

dry vermouth: A fortified white wine, usually 18 percent alcohol (36 proof), that contains at most 5 percent residual sugar. It's consumed as an aperitif and is a vital part of the Dry Martini.

Elixir Végétal: Made from the same base of about 130 medicinal and aromatic plants and flowers as Chartreuse but far stronger. It can be described as a cordial or a liqueur and is claimed to be a tonic. Sold in small bottles placed in wooden casing.

falernum: A sweet syrup used in Caribbean and tropical drinks. It contains flavours of almond, ginger and/or cloves, lime, and sometimes vanilla or allspice.

fat washing: A method of infusing liquor with a fatty product, usually meat.

Fernet-Branca: Long known as a digestif, it originated in Milan in the early 1800s. As with most such elixirs, it is made from a secret formula. This one purportedly includes some 40 ingredients, including rhubarb, chamomile, and myrrh.

fino sherry: A pale, very dry sherry produced in Jerez, Spain.

fizz: A type of mixed drink; a variation on the older sours family. The defining features of the fizz are an acidic juice (such as lemon or lime juice) and carbonated water.

flip: A chilled, creamy drink made with eggs, sugar, and a wine or spirit (brandy and sherry are two of the most common choices).

float: (verb/noun) Adding a liquid or foam to a drink without turbulence or mixing. The addition should be a distinct layer sitting on top of the other components of the cocktail.

foam: Foams can be made a few different ways using Versawhip or egg whites. You can shake the foam with ice and the cocktail to create a frothy drink, or you can make it separately in a whipped cream canister and then add it to the top of the drink. The addition of flavours to foams, egg white or other, adds a new texture and dimension to a drink because the cocktail is sipped through the flavoured foam.

Frangelico: A hazelnut and herbal liqueur produced in Canale, Italy. It is 20 percent abv, 40 proof. It was released in the 1980s, gaining attention largely because of its unusual packaging—its bottle was designed to look like a friar, complete with a knotted white cord around the waist. Frangelico is made in a similar manner to some other nut liqueurs. Nut meats are crumbled up and combined with cocoa, vanilla berries, and other natural flavours, then left to soak in the base spirit. After the spirit has absorbed the flavour of the ingredients, the liqueur is filtered, sweetened, and bottled.

Galliano: A sweet herbal liqueur created in 1896 by Italian distiller and brandy producer Arturo Vaccari of Livorno, Tuscany, and named after Giuseppe Galliano, an Italian hero of the First Italo-Ethiopian War. Its vivid yellow colour symbolizes the gold rushes of the 1890s. Galliano has a large number of natural ingredients including vanilla, star anise, Mediterranean anise, ginger, citrus, juniper, musk yarrow, and lavender. Neutral alcohol is infused with the pressings from all the herbs except vanilla. The liquid is then distilled and infused with pressed vanilla. In the final stage, distilled water, refined sugar, and pure neutral alcohol are blended with the base.

gentian: The roots of a yellow-petalled flower found in southern Europe that are dried and used as a tonic, stomachic, and flavouring in vermouth.

ginger disc: A thin slice of ginger resembling a disc.

gold rum: Rum that has been aged in oak barrels, which give it a golden colour. Usually has a slightly deeper and more complex flavour than white rum. Also called amber rum.

gomme syrup: Rich simple sugar syrup with the addition of gum arabic.

grenadine: A red syrup created by combining various berry juices and sugar. Most commonly, though, pomegranate juice is the main ingredient.

gum arabic: The hardened sap from Acacia trees. Used as a stabilizer and thickening agent. Also known as acacia gum.

Heering Cherry: Danish cherry liqueur that has been made since 1818. Used most notably in the Singapore Sling and the Blood & Sand.

Herbsaint: Herbsaint first appeared in 1934. It was the creation of J. Marion Legendre and Reginald Parker of New Orleans, who had learned how to make absinthe while in France during the First World War. It first went on sale as a substitute for absinthe following the repeal of Prohibition. Herbsaint was originally produced under the name "Legendre Absinthe", although it never contained grand wormwood (*Artemisia absinthium*). The Federal Alcohol Control Administration soon objected to Legendre's use of the word "absinthe," so the name was changed to "Legendre Herbsaint." The Sazerac Company bought J.M. Legendre & Co. in June

1949. Herbsaint was bottled at 120 proof and 100 proof for many years. But when the recipe was modified in the mid-1950s, it was bottled at 100 proof and 90 proof. By the early 1970s, the 100-proof variation was discontinued and the 90-proof version remains the predominant Herbsaint available today. In December 2009, the Sazerac Company reintroduced J.M. Legendre's original 100 proof recipe as Herbsaint Original. The name Herbsaint originates from *herbe sainte* (sacred herb), the French/Creole term for *Artemisia absinthium*.

housemade: (adjective) Anything that's been made by the bar for use in drinks. Specialty syrups and liqueurs are often housemade.

Hpnotiq: A fruit juice liqueur with a base of vodka and cognac. Native to New York but produced in France by Heaven Hill Distilleries.

ice globe: Ice shaped into a globe or sphere using a specialty mould, carving technique, or ice globe press.

infuse: (verb) To let ingredients sit in alcohol for a prolonged period of time, allowing flavours to release into the liquid.

Islay whisky: Home to only nine distilleries, Islay is one of the smaller of the Scottish whisky regions. It produces notably smokier whiskies than other regions due to the use of local peat to smoke the malts.

kirsch: A clear, colourless fruit brandy traditionally made from a double distillation of Morello cherries. It can, however, be made from other varieties. The cherries are fermented completely, even the pits. Good-quality kirsch has a dry cherry flavour with a slightly bitter almond taste.

kola nut powder: The powder derived from the nuts of the cola trees of Africa. One of the original caffeine and flavour ingredients in old-school colas.

Last Word: A gin-based Prohibition-era cocktail written about by Ted Saucier, a Canadian icon in the cocktail scene. A mix of equal parts gin, maraschino, Green Chartreuse, and lime juice. The drink was resurrected by Murray Stenson in Seattle.

Lillet Blanc: Lillet is a brand of French aperitif wine. It is a blend of 85 percent Bordeaux wines (Sauvignon Blanc, Sémillon, and Muscadelle) and 15 percent macerated liqueurs—mostly citrus liqueurs made from the peels of sweet oranges from Spain and Morocco as well as bitter green oranges from Haiti. Lillet belongs to a family of aperitifs known as tonic wines because of the addition of a liqueur of cinchona bark from Peru, which contains quinine. Lillet is matured in oak casks and available in red, white, and rosé versions. While it had been produced since the late nineteenth century under the name Kina Lillet, the current formulation, called Lillet Blanc, dates from 1986, when the recipe was changed to lower the sugar content and bitterness.

London dry gin: The most classic style of gin available, resulting from the infusion and redistillation of various botanicals, with juniper berries being predominant.

madeira: A proprietary fortified wine from Madeira, Portugal. Madeira can be made in two styles: Dry aperitif or sweeter dessert. It is produced using the unique *estufagem* aging process, which is meant to duplicate the effect of a long sea voyage through tropical climates on the aging barrels.

Mai Tai: It was purportedly invented in 1944 at the Trader Vic's restaurant in Oakland, California. Trader Vic's rival, Don the Beachcomber, claimed to have created it in 1933 at his then new Hollywood bar, which he named after himself. (It is now a famous restaurant.) Don the Beachcomber's recipe is more complex than Vic's and tastes quite different. The Trader Vic story of its invention is that the Trader (Victor J. Bergeron) created it one afternoon for some friends who were visiting from Tahiti. One of those friends, Carrie Guild, tasted it and cried out, *"Maita'i roa ae!"* (literally "very good!" figuratively "Out of this world! The best!"). Hence the name. It's a mix of rums, curaçao, and lime juice.

Manhattan: The classic and most well-known New York borough cocktail uses a mix of rye, sweet vermouth, and bitters. Classically, Abbott's Bitters were used, but Angostura bitters are more common now.

metheglin mead: Metheglin is traditional mead (honey wine) with added herbs and/or spices. Some of the most common metheglins contain ginger, tea, orange peel, nutmeg, coriander, cinnamon, cloves, or vanilla. Many metheglins were originally employed as folk medicines. The Welsh word for mead is *medd*, and the word "metheglin" derives from *meddyglyn*, a compound of *meddyg* (healing) and *llyn* (liquor).

mezcal: An agave spirit mostly made in Oaxaca, Mexico, using a variety of pit-roasted agave plants. Mezcal is still produced by the same distillation process that has been used for centuries. It often has rich smoky, earthy tones that set it apart from Jalisco's agave spirit, tequila.

Negroni: Created in the early 1900s in Italy, the Negroni is a classic Italian aperitif made with equal parts gin, sweet vermouth, and Campari.

neutral grain spirit: A colourless and tasteless liquid distilled from grain mash to 95 percent abv.

New Western dry gin: A style of gin that emerged only in the last few years, following the explosion in the number of distilleries in the Pacific Northwest. Usually contains specialty botanicals only found in the region. The term was coined by Ryan Magarian of Aviation Gin.

Old Fashioned: The Old-Fashioned cocktail is one of the originals that defined classic cocktails. It's a mix of whiskey (usually bourbon or rye), bitters, and a sugar cube stirred with ice and garnished with a twist of orange or lemon.

Old Pal: A mix of rye, dry vermouth, and Campari. This cocktail first appeared in Harry MacElhone's 1922 book *Harry's ABC of Mixing Cocktails*. He claims the drink was invented by Sparrow Robertson, the then-sporting editor for the *New York Herald*'s office in Paris. It's possible the drink fell out of MacElhone's repertoire by 1927 as it did not appear in his next book, *Barflies and Cocktails*. Instead, he swapped the rye for bourbon whiskey and the dry vermouth for sweet and renamed the drink "The Boulevardier." The recipe for the Old Pal was published again in Harry Craddock's 1930 cocktail book *The Savoy Cocktail Book*.

oloroso sherry: A Spanish

fortified wine. Its production method allows for heavy oxidization, causing the flavours to be deep and nutty.

orange bitters: Traditionally this liquid is citrusy and slightly bitter, like orange peel.

orgeat syrup: Sweet syrup made from almonds and sugar, with rose water or orange flower water added.

overproof rum: Rum distilled to have a higher abv, usually in the 60 to 75 percent range. Comes in white and aged styles.

Perlini: A relatively new system consisting of a special pressurized shaker that lets bartenders carbonate any liquid they wish. It was created by Perlage (famous for their wine and champagne preservation system).

Peychaud's bitters: Gentian-based bitters with a lighter body, sweeter taste, and more floral aroma than other bitters which cannot be substituted. First made around 1830 by Antoine Amédée Peychaud, a Creole pharmacist/apothecary from the French colony of Saint-Domingue (now called Haiti) who settled in New Orleans in 1795.

picked: (adjective) A small piece of fruit or vegetable pierced through with a cocktail pick.

pimento dram: A rum-based allspice berry liqueur from the Caribbean. Also known as allspice dram.

Pimm's: Pimm's or Pimm's No. 1 (the most available version) is a gin-based fruit cup or liqueur that was created in 1823 by James Pimm in London for use at his oyster bar. Originally there were different cups which used different base spirits. For example, No. 2 was Scotch-based.

pisco: A brandy that can only be made in Chile or Peru using government-controlled grape varieties and particular distillation methods, it is distilled to proof and aged slightly before bottling.

pommeau: A liquor made by mixing apple must (unfermented cider) and aged calvados which is sometimes aged after blending.

PolyScience Smoking Gun: A modern piece of equipment that enables you to cold smoke anything. The traditional method of smoking puts heat to wood chips or other woody substances, which limits what you can smoke because things like liquor cannot have direct heat applied to them for as long as is needed for smoking. The PolyScience Smoking Gun is actually a very simple piece of an equipment. It consists of an electric fan, a small hopper in which to place wood chips or smoking material, and a tube to pump the smoke into the liquid. The fan blows cool air through the hopper, and the lit material inside, and down the tube.

powdered sugar: Finely-ground

sugar that's similar to icing sugar without the cream of tartar that is added as a thickening agent.

prosecco: Generally, a dry or extra-dry Italian sparkling wine.

quinquina: A collective name for bitters and fortified wines with quinine (Peruvian Bark) as the main ingredient.

reposado tequila: Tequila that has been aged for six to 18 months in oak barrels (usually old bourbon barrels).

Rickey: A cocktail similar to a fizz but using lime juice and soda.

rose water: A by-product of rose petals that are distilled to extract the oils for perfume. Adds a very floral tone to drinks.

rye whiskey: In the United States, rye whiskey must be made from a mash of at least 51 percent rye, with the rest of the mash made up of corn, barley, etc. In Canada, there is no law as to how much rye needs to be added, so the term Canadian whisky is truer than calling it rye.

Saskatoon berry: Native to the Canadian Prairies and as far west as the coast of British Columbia, it is similar to the blueberry in appearance and taste, but with a hint of wild fruit flavour as well.

Sazerac: The Sazerac is a local New Orleans variation of an Old Fashioned cognac or whisky cocktail, named for the Sazerac de Forge et Fils brand of cognac that was its original primary ingredient. The drink is made from some combination of cognac or rye whisky, absinthe or Herbsaint, and Peychaud's bitters; it is distinguished by its preparation method. In 2008, Congress passed a motion naming the Sazerac the official drink of New Orleans, one of the first cocktails to ever get the designation in the United States.

schnapps: A strong, clear alcohol that can be flavoured with a variety of different ingredients. Popular choices include apple, peppermint, and peach.

shrub: Popular during America's colonial era, the shrub is a simple mixture of fruit, sugar, and vinegar. (In eighteenth-century England, where they originated, shrubs were fortified with liquor such as rum or brandy.)

smoking: A new method of adding flavour to a drink using a PolyScience Smoking Gun. Smoking lets bartenders infuse cold smoke into a liquid in a manner of minutes without exposing it to direct heat.

SodaStream Bottle: A simple little piece of equipment that uses a CO_2 tank to infuse the liquid in the pressurized bottle with the gas, carbonating it.

solera: A process for aging liquids in which a succession of containers is filled with product over a series of equal aging intervals (usually each a year). One container is filled for each interval. At the end of the intervals, after the last container is filled, the oldest container is tapped for part of its content, which is bottled. Then that container is refilled from the next oldest container, and that one in succession from the third oldest, down to the youngest container, which is refilled with new product. This procedure is repeated at the end of each aging interval. The transferred product mixes with the older product in the next container.

sour: A classic sour cocktail uses lemon, lime, or any sour citrus to "sour" the drink. Usually, it is a simple mix of spirit, sugar, and sour, sometimes with the addition of egg white.

spiced rum: A classic rum style featuring added and infused spices, such as cinnamon, cloves, vanilla, and nutmeg.

sprig: A small twig or shoot garnish, most commonly fresh mint, basil, or rosemary.

spritz: A classic style of drink that uses soda or prosecco as an effervescent element, such as Aperol Spritz.

Strega: An Italian herbal liqueur produced since 1860 by the S.A. Distilleria Liquore Strega, it contains about 70 herbal ingredients, including mint, fennel, and saffron, the latter giving it its yellow colour. Strega means "witch" in Italian.

sweet vermouth: A white (bianco) or red (rosso) fortified wine which is usually 15 to 16 percent alcohol (30–32 proof) and containing up to 15 percent sugar, it is used as an aperitif as well as in slightly-sweet cocktails such as the Manhattan.

switchel: A refreshing drink that originated in the Caribbean and is made from ginger, molasses, apple cider vinegar, sugar, and water. It was very popular in the American colonies in the seventeenth century.

swizzle: (verb) To whisk or blend liquor and crushed ice together in a glass.

swizzle: (noun) A cocktail family, usually rum-based drinks with crushed ice, that traditionally was swizzled with a small branch that had four to five stalks at the end. Today, you can use a simple stick (such as a chopstick) to achieve the same effect.

Szechuan peppercorns: A common spice in Asian cooking.

Tennessee whiskey: Very similar to bourbon whiskey except made in Tennessee, usually using the sour mash method of fermentation.

tincture: An alcoholic extract of plant or animal material or a solution with 40 to 60 percent abv.

Toronto: First published in Robert Vermeire's 1922 cocktail book *Cocktails—How to Mix Them* as the Fernet

Cocktail with the quote, "This cocktail is much appreciated by the Canadians of Toronto." It was later published in David Embury's 1948 cocktail book *The Fine Art of Mixing Drinks* and listed as the Toronto Cocktail. It is a mix of Canadian whisky, Fernet-Branca, sugar, and Angostura bitters.

Tuaca Liqueur: A brandy-based liqueur with orange and predominantly vanilla flavours. Originally made in Italy, it is now manufactured in the United States.

turbinado sugar: A style of brown sugar made by spinning molasses in a centrifuge and cooling it into crystals.

Versawhip: Pure, enzymatically treated soy protein that can be hydrated with water and whipped to make a foam.

White Lady: Another classic from Harry McElhone, it is a refreshing blend of gin, Cointreau, and lemon juice with an optional egg white.

white rum: A common style of rum that has not been aged in a barrel or has been aged for no more than six months and then filtered.

wormwood (*Artemisia absinthium*): An ingredient in absinthe, it is also used for flavouring some other spirits and wines, including bitters, vermouth, and Chartreuse.

xanthan gum: A natural, gluten-free carbohydrate produced by fermenting glucose with a bacterium called *Xanthomonas campestris*, which is harmful to plants such as cabbage.

ABOUT SHAWN SOOLE

What began as a youthful ambition to craft the perfect cocktail has matured into a proficiency across every aspect of beverage service. Twenty years after being named State Title winner by the Australian Bartenders Guild, Shawn Soole continues to view the service industry as a medium to deliver his unique style of exceptional customer experience.

From bar/restaurant concept creation, menu formulation, staff training, and launch guidance, to branding, marketing, and public relations strategies, Shawn's experience and advancement of the industry has been prolific. He has co-authored the books *Cocktail Culture* (2013) and *Great Northern Cocktails* (2019) as well as providing ongoing contributions to publications such as *Liquor.com* and *EAT Magazine.*

As a dedicated and vocal proponent of the industry, Shawn has presented keynote speeches (Lisbon Bar Show), increased public awareness for distillers in BC, Canada (BC Spirits) and continues to advocate his mission 'to make the industry better for everyone'. His input has been vital to the launch and/or ongoing success of numerous highly acclaimed bar and beverage programs, such as Little Jumbo in 2013, OLO in 2015, Café Mexico in 2016, and in 2018, Pagliacci's.

To accommodate his growing role as a consultant, Shawn founded Soole Hospitality Concepts (SHC)—a network of industry leaders with decades of multi-faceted experience. Together they provide innovative responses to all the needs of hospitality-oriented businesses. His firm belief in the importance of consistent personal growth drove him to recently complete a diploma in Advanced Hospitality and Tourism Management at Camosun College, achieving a level of distinction that placed him on the Dean's List.

His latest undertaking is the conceptual development, systems implementation, and launch guidance for Miss Fitz and Roxy, two bars under the SOS Group banner in Singapore.

CPSIA information can be obtained
at www.ICGtesting.com
Printed in the USA
LVHW02054530 1019
635745LV00001B/1

9 781907 434525